W9-AUC-844

LEVEL I REFRESHER: CONTENTS

SCHWESERNOTES™ 2012 CFA LEVEL I REFRESHER

©2011 Kaplan, Inc. All rights reserved.

Published in 2011 by Kaplan Schweser.

Printed in the United States of America.

ISBN: 978-1-4277-3607-9 / 1-4277-3607-3

PPN: 3200-1734

FOREWORD

The Level I Refresher is a review of the topics from Level I that provide a foundation for Level II—topics that the writers of the 2012 Level II exam assume you are familiar with when you study for and then sit for the exam. Our intention in this book is to show you how those concepts relate to material in the Level II curriculum. For example, the Level II quantitative methods material assumes that you remember hypothesis testing from Level I. To set you up for success at Level II, the Level I Refresher contains a thorough review of the key quantitative methods, economics, financial reporting and analysis, corporate finance, fixed income, derivatives, and portfolio management concepts from Level I.

You will see concepts on the Level II exam that you saw at Level I, but they will be tested from a different perspective or in more detail. Remember, Level I is all about foundation and Level II is all about valuation. Your understanding of how all 18 of the Level II study sessions relate to one another is much more vital than it was at Level I.

As you read through this book, it may seem like there is a great quantity of review material, and there is—nearly all the 2012 Level II study sessions are represented. This is because a majority of the material at Level II builds on material from Level I. For example, the derivatives material at Level II assumes that you remember the payoffs to call and put options and can apply that knowledge to value those options.

It is important to mention that the format of the Level II exam is different from that of Level I. The Level II exam is made up of 20 item sets—vignettes followed by six multiple-choice questions that draw on the information in that vignette. There are 10 item sets in the morning session and 10 item sets in the afternoon session, for a total of 120 questions worth three points each. You will not see Level I concepts tested at Level II, but an understanding of Level I concepts is necessary to master the Level II concepts you need to be successful at Level II.

The Level II CFA exam is a grueling mental, as well as physical, challenge that is not to be taken lightly. However, your hard work and dedication combined with our high-quality study materials are your keys to exam day success. We wish you all the best for your studies at Level II.

Bijesh Tolia

Dr. Bijesh Tolia, CFA
VP and CFA Level II Manager

Kaplan Schweser

LEVEL I REFRESHER

ETHICS (STUDY SESSIONS 1 & 2)

At Level II, your knowledge of the ethics material remains extremely important to your overall success on the exam. The core of the ethics material, the Code and Standards, remains the same as it was at Level I, so we recommend spending about 80% of your ethics study time on the Standards of Professional Conduct. However, there are two important differences in ethics from Level I. At Level II:

- There is a second ethics study session (#2) that contains some additional readings that may be tested, including the CFA Institute Soft Dollar Standards, the CFA Institute Research Objectivity Standards, and the New Prudent Investor Rule. Spend the other 20% of your ethics study time on these topics.
- There are no LOS related to Global Investment Performance Standards (GIPS®).

©2011 Kaplan, Inc.

QUANTITATIVE METHODS (STUDY SESSION 3)

The Time Value of Money

While there are no specific time value of money (TVM) LOS in the Level II curriculum, the concept is important because it integrates with many other Level II topics. Any Level II concepts that involve discounting cash flows for valuation require TVM calculations. In corporate finance, you need to value expansion and replacement projects; in equity, you need to use equity dividend discount, free cash flow, and residual income models to value equity investments. You will also value real estate investments. TVM concepts also appear in the callable bond valuation and swap valuation material. No matter where TVM shows up on the exam, the key to any TVM problem is to draw a time line and determine when the cash flows occur so you can discount the cash flows appropriately.

Basic TVM Terminology

Future value (FV) is the amount to which an investment grows after one or more compounding periods.

- *Compounding* is the process used to determine the future value of a current amount.
- The *periodic rate* is the nominal rate (stated in annual terms) divided by the number of compounding periods (e.g., for quarterly compounding, divide the annual rate by four).
- The *number of compounding periods* is equal to the number of years multiplied by the frequency of compounding (e.g., for quarterly compounding, multiply the number of years by four).

$$\text{future value} = \text{present value} \times (1 + \text{periodic rate})^{\text{number of compounding periods}}$$

Level I Refresher

Present value (PV) is the current value of some future cash flow.

- *Discounting* is the process used to determine the present value of some future amount.
- *Discount rate* is the periodic rate used in the discounting process.

$$\text{present value} = \frac{\text{future value}}{(1 + \text{periodic rate})^{\text{number of compounding periods}}}$$

For *non-annual compounding problems*, divide the interest rate by the number of compounding periods per year, *m*, and multiply the number of years by the number of compounding periods per year.

An annuity is a stream of equal cash flows that occurs at equal intervals over a given period. A corporate bond combines an annuity (the equal semiannual coupon payments) with a lump-sum payment (return of principal at maturity).

- *Ordinary annuity.* Cash flows occur at the end of each compounding period.
- *Annuity due.* Cash flows occur at the beginning of each period.

Present value of an ordinary annuity. Answers the question, "How much would an annuity of $X every (month, week, quarter, year) cost today if the periodic rate is *I*%?"

The present value of an annuity is just the sum of the present values of all the payments. Your calculator will do this for you.

- N = number of periods.
- I/Y = interest rate per period.
- PMT = amount of each periodic payment.
- FV = 0.
- Compute (CPT) present value (PV).

Future value of an ordinary annuity. Just change to PV = 0 and CPT → FV.

If there is a mismatch between the period of the payments and the period for the interest rate, adjust the interest rate to match. Do not add or divide payment amounts. If you have a *monthly payment,* you need a *monthly interest rate.*

Present and Future Value of an Annuity Due

$$PV_{\text{annuity due}} = PV_{\text{ordinary annuity}} \times (1 + \text{periodic rate})$$

$$FV_{\text{annuity due}} = FV_{\text{ordinary annuity}} \times (1 + \text{periodic rate})$$

Once you have found the PV (FV) of an ordinary annuity, you can convert the discounted (compound) value to an annuity due value by multiplying by one plus the periodic rate. This effectively discounts (compounds) the ordinary annuity value by one less (more) period.

Perpetuities are annuities with infinite lives:

$$PV_{perpetuity} = \frac{periodic\ payment}{periodic\ interest\ rate}$$

Preferred stock is an example of a perpetuity (equal payments indefinitely).

Present (future) value of any series of cash flows is equal to the sum of the present (future) values of each cash flow. This means you can break up cash flows any way that is convenient, take the PV or FV of the pieces, and add them up to get the PV or FV of the whole series of cash flows.

DISCOUNTED CASH FLOW AND YIELD APPLICATIONS

This material has direct application to Level II, particularly Study Session 8 in Corporate Finance, as well as nearly all of the equity material. On exam day, you need to be completely comfortable with the mechanics of discounted cash flow calculations. This section also reviews simple yield calculations.

NPV of an Investment Project

- *Identify* all outflows/inflows associated with the investment.
- *Determine* discount rate appropriate for the investment.
- *Find PV* of each cash flow. Inflows are positive and increase NPV.
- Outflows are negative and decrease NPV. There is usually a net investment (negative cash flow) at time zero to begin the project.
- *Compute* NPV, the sum of all the discounted cash flows.

$$NPV = \frac{CF_1}{(1+r)} + \frac{CF_2}{(1+r)^2} + ... + \frac{CF_{t-1}}{(1+r)^{t-1}} + \frac{CF_t}{(1+r)^t} - NI$$

CF_t = expected net cash flow at time *t*
r = discount rate = opportunity cost of capital
NI = net (time = 0) investment in the project

With uneven cash flows, use the CF function.

Computing IRR

IRR is the discount rate that equates the PV of the cash inflows with the PV of the cash outflows. This also makes IRR the discount rate that results in NPV equal to zero. In other words, the IRR is the r that, when plugged into the previous NPV equation, makes the NPV equal zero.

When given a set of equal cash inflows, such as an annuity, calculate IRR by solving for I/Y.

When the cash inflows are uneven, use the CF function on your calculator.

Example:

Project cost is $100, CF_1 = $50, CF_2 = $50, and CF_3 = $90. What is the NPV at 10%? What is the IRR of the project?

Answer:

Enter CF0 = –100, C01 = 50, F01 = 2, C02 = 90, F02 = 1.

NPV, 10, enter, ↓, CPT, display 54.395.

IRR, CPT, display 35.71 (%).

NPV vs. IRR

- *NPV decision rule:* For independent projects, adopt all projects with NPV > 0. These projects will increase the value of the firm.
- *IRR decision rule:* For independent projects, adopt all projects with IRR > required project return. These projects will also add value to the firm.

NPV and IRR rules give the same decision for independent projects.

When NPV and IRR rankings differ, rely on NPV for choosing between or among projects.

YIELD CALCULATIONS

Bond-equivalent yield is two times the semiannually compounded yield. This is because U.S. bonds pay interest semiannually rather than annually.

Yield to maturity (YTM) is the IRR on a bond. For a semiannual coupon bond, YTM is two times semiannual IRR. In other words, it is the discount rate that equates the present value of a bond's cash flows with its market price. We will revisit this topic again in the fixed income section.

Holding period yield (HPY), also called holding period return (HPR):

$$\text{holding period yield} = \text{HPY} = \frac{P_1 - P_0 + D_1}{P_0} \text{ or } \frac{P_1 + D_1}{P_0} - 1$$

For common stocks, the cash distribution (D_1) is the dividend. For bonds, the cash distribution is the interest payment.

HPR for a given investment can be calculated for any time period (day, week, month, or year) simply by changing the end points of the time interval over which values and cash flows are measured.

STATISTICAL CONCEPTS AND MARKET RETURNS

You need to understand the measures of central tendency material in quantitative methods. The concepts of the expected holding period return and expected percentage change appear in numerous LOS throughout the Level II curriculum, particularly in equity. Knowing how to calculate an expected portfolio return is covered in portfolio management. The Sharpe ratio is used in portfolio management.

Measures of Central Tendency

Arithmetic mean. A population average is called the population mean (denoted μ). The average of a sample (subset of a population) is called the sample mean (denoted $\bar{x}$). Both the population and sample means are calculated as arithmetic means (simple average). We use the sample mean as a best guess approximation of the population mean.

Median. Middle value of a data set, half above and half below. With an even number of observations, median is the average of the two middle observations.

Mode. Value occurring most frequently in a data set. Data sets can have more than one mode (bimodal, trimodal, etc.) but only one mean and one median.

Level I Refresher

Geometric mean:

- Used to calculate compound growth rates.
- If returns are constant over time, geometric mean equals arithmetic mean.
- The greater the variability of returns over time, the greater the difference between arithmetic and geometric mean (arithmetic will always be higher).
- When calculating the geometric mean for a returns series, it is necessary to add one to each value under the radical and then subtract one from the result.
- The geometric mean is used to calculate the time-weighted return, a performance measure.

$$\text{geometric mean return} = R_G = \sqrt[n]{(1+R_1)\times(1+R_2)\times...\times(1+R_n)} - 1$$

Example:

A mutual fund had the following returns for the past three years: 15%, –9%, and 13%. What is the arithmetic mean return, the 3-year holding period return, and the average annual compound (geometric mean) return?

Answer:

$$\text{arithmetic mean: } \frac{15\% - 9\% + 13\%}{3} = 6.333\%$$

$$\text{holding period return: } 1.15\times0.91\times1.13 - 1 = 0.183 = 18.3\%$$

$$\text{geometric mean: } R_G = \sqrt[3]{(1+0.15)\times(1-0.09)\times(1+0.13)} - 1$$
$$= \sqrt[3]{1.183} - 1 = 1.0575 - 1 = 0.0575 = 5.75\%$$

Geometric mean return is useful for finding the yield on a zero-coupon bond with a maturity of several years or for finding the average annual growth rate of a company's dividend or earnings across several years. Geometric mean returns are a compound return measure.

Weighted mean. Mean in which different observations are given different proportional influence on the mean:

$$\text{weighted mean} = \overline{X}_w = \sum_{i=1}^{n} w_i X_i = \left(w_1 X_1 + w_2 X_2 + ... + w_n X_n \right)$$

where:

$X_1, X_2, ..., X_n$ = observed values

$w_1, w_2, ..., w_n$ = corresponding weights for each observation, $\sum w_i = 1$

Weighted means are used to calculate the actual or expected return on a portfolio, given the actual or expected returns for each portfolio asset (or asset class). For portfolio returns, the weights in the formula are the percentages of the total portfolio value invested in each asset (or asset class).

Example: Portfolio return

A portfolio is 20% invested in Stock A, 30% invested in Stock B, and 50% invested in Stock C. Stocks A, B, and C experienced returns of 10%, 15%, and 3%, respectively. Calculate the portfolio return.

Answer:

$$R_p = 0.2(10\%) + 0.3(15\%) + 0.5(3\%) = 8.0\%$$

A weighted mean is also used to calculate the expected return given a probability model. The weights are the probabilities of each outcome.

Example: Expected portfolio return

A portfolio of stocks has a 15% probability of achieving a 35% return, a 25% chance of achieving a 15% return, and a 60% chance of achieving a 10% return. Calculate the expected portfolio return.

Answer:

$$E(R_p) = 0.15(35) + 0.25(15) + 0.60(10) = 5.25 + 3.75 + 6 = 15\%$$

Note that an arithmetic mean is a weighted mean in which all of the weights are equal to 1/n (where *n* is the number of observations).

Measures of Dispersion

Range is the difference between the largest and smallest value in a data set and is the simplest measure of dispersion. You can think of the dispersion as measuring the width of the distribution. The narrower the range, the less dispersion.

Variance is defined as the average of the squared deviations from the mean.

Example:

Stocks A, B, and C had returns of 10%, 30%, and 20%, respectively. Calculate the population variance (denoted σ^2) and sample variance (denoted s^2).

Answer:

The process begins the same for population and sample variance.

Step 1: Calculate the mean (expected return): $\dfrac{(10+30+20)}{3} = 20$

Step 2: Calculate the squared deviations from the mean and add them together:

$$(10-20)^2 + (30-20)^2 + (20-20)^2 = 100+100+0 = 200$$

Step 3: Divide by number of observations (n = 3) for the population variance and by the number of observations minus one for the sample variance:

$$\text{population variance} = \sigma^2 = \frac{200}{3} = 66.67$$

$$\text{sample variance} = s^2 = \frac{200}{3-1} = \frac{200}{2} = 100$$

$$\sigma^2 = \frac{\sum\limits_{i=1}^{N}(X_i - \mu)^2}{N} \qquad s^2 = \frac{\sum\limits_{i=1}^{n}(X_i - \overline{X})^2}{n-1}$$

©2011 Kaplan, Inc.

Standard deviation is the square root of variance. On the exam, if the question is asking for the standard deviation, do not forget to take the square root!

Coefficient of variation expresses how much dispersion exists relative to the mean of a distribution and allows for direct comparison of the degree of dispersion across different data sets. It measures risk per unit of expected return.

$$CV = \frac{\text{standard deviation of returns}}{\text{mean return}}$$

When comparing two investments using the CV criterion, the one with the lower CV is the better choice.

The *Sharpe ratio* is widely used to evaluate investment performance and measures excess return per unit of risk. Portfolios with large Sharpe ratios are preferred to portfolios with smaller ratios because it is assumed that rational investors prefer higher excess returns (i.e., returns in excess of the risk-free rate) and dislike risk.

$$\text{Sharpe ratio} = \frac{\text{excess return}}{\text{risk}} = \frac{R_{\text{portfolio}} - R_{\text{risk-free}}}{\sigma_p}$$

COMMON PROBABILITY DISTRIBUTIONS

This material (from this point on to the end of quantitative methods) is background for hypothesis testing, which is no longer a separate topic in the Level II curriculum. However, the material on multiple regression assumes that you understand and can apply hypothesis testing to the correlation coefficient and the population parameter for a regression coefficient. The material on the safety-first ratio is an extension of the Sharpe ratio material in the previous section. The concept of continuous compounding is useful in derivatives. The concept of lognormal distributions is important for the Level II time series material.

Normal Distribution: Properties

- Completely described by mean and variance.
- Symmetric about the mean (skewness = 0).
- Kurtosis (a measure of peakedness) = 3.
- Linear combination of jointly, normally distributed random variables is also normally distributed.

Many properties of the normal distribution are evident from examining the graph of a normal distribution's probability density function:

Figure 1: Normal Distribution Probability Density Function

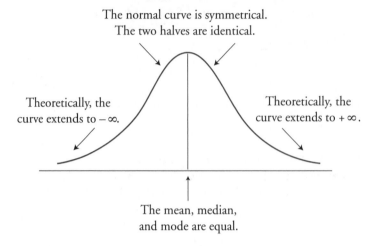

Calculating Probabilities Using the Standard Normal Distribution

The *z-value* standardizes an observation from a normal distribution and represents the number of standard deviations a given observation is from the population mean.

$$z = \frac{\text{observation} - \text{population mean}}{\text{standard deviation}} = \frac{x - \mu}{\sigma}$$

Confidence Intervals: Normal Distribution

A *confidence interval* is a range of values around an expected outcome within which we expect the actual outcome to occur some specified percentage of the time.

The following graph illustrates confidence intervals for a standard normal distribution, which has a mean of 0 and a standard deviation of 1. We can interpret the values on the x-axis as the number of standard deviations from the mean. Thus, for any normal distribution we can say, for example, that 68% of the outcomes will be within one standard deviation of the mean. This would be referred to as a 68% confidence interval.

Figure 2: The Standard Normal Distribution and Confidence Intervals

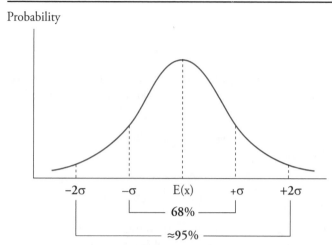

Consider a normal distribution with mean μ and standard deviation σ. Each observation has an expected value of μ. If we draw a sample of size n from the distribution, the mean of the sample has an expected value of μ. The larger the sample, the closer to μ we expect the sample mean to be. The standard deviation of the means of samples of size n is simply $\sigma/\sqrt{n}$ and is called *standard error of the sample mean*. This allows us to construct a confidence interval for the sample mean for a sample of size n.

Example:

Calculate a 95% confidence interval for the mean of a sample of size 25 drawn from a normal distribution with a mean of 8 and standard deviation of 4.

Answer:

The standard deviation of sample means for samples of size 25 is:

$$\frac{4}{\sqrt{25}} = \frac{4}{5} = 0.8$$

A 95% confidence interval will extend 1.96 standard deviations above and below the mean, so our 95% confidence interval is:

$$8 \pm 1.96 \times 0.8 = 6.432 \text{ to } 9.568$$

We believe the mean of a sample of 25 observations will fall within this interval 95% of the time.

With a known variance, the formula for a confidence interval is:

$$\bar{x} \pm z_{\alpha/2} \frac{\sigma}{\sqrt{n}}$$

In other words, the confidence interval is equal to the mean value, plus or minus the z-score that corresponds to the given significance level multiplied by the standard error.

- Confidence intervals and z-scores are very important in hypothesis testing, a topic that will be reviewed shortly.

Lognormal Distribution

If x is normally distributed, $Y = e^x$ is lognormally distributed. Values of a lognormal distribution are always positive, so it is used to model asset prices (rather than rates of return, which can be negative). The lognormal distribution is positively skewed, as shown in the following figure.

Figure 3: Lognormal Distribution

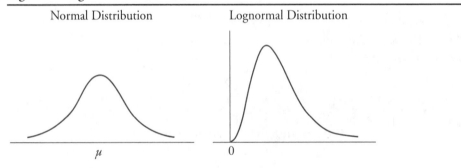

Continuously Compounded Returns

If we increase the number of compounding periods (n) for an annual rate of return, the limit as n goes toward infinity is continuous compounding. For a specific holding period return (HPR), the relation to the continuously compounded return over the holding period (CCR) is as follows:

$$CCR = \ln(1+HPR) = \ln\left(\frac{\text{ending value}}{\text{beginning value}}\right)$$

$$HPR = \frac{\text{ending value}}{\text{beginning value}} - 1 = e^{CCR} - 1$$

When the holding period is one year, so that HPR is also the effective annual return, CCR is the annual continuously compounded rate of return.

Simulation

Historical simulation of outcomes (e.g., changes in portfolio values) is done by randomly selecting changes in price or risk factors from actual (historical) past changes in these factors and modeling the effects of these changes on the value of a current portfolio. The results of historical simulation have limitations because future changes may not necessarily be distributed as past changes were.

Monte Carlo simulation is performed by making assumptions about the distributions of prices or risk factors and using a large number of computer-generated random values for the relevant risk factors or prices to generate a distribution of possible outcomes (e.g., project NPVs, portfolio values). The simulated distributions can only be as accurate as the assumptions about the distributions of and correlations between the input variables assumed in the procedure.

SAMPLING AND ESTIMATION

Central Limit Theorem

The *central limit theorem* of statistics states that in selecting simple random samples of size n from a population with a mean μ and a finite variance σ^2, the sampling distribution of the sample mean approaches a normal probability distribution with mean μ and a variance equal to σ^2/n as the sample size becomes large.

The central limit theorem is extremely useful because the normal distribution is relatively easy to apply to hypothesis testing and to the construction of confidence intervals.

Specific inferences about the population mean can be made from the sample mean, *regardless of the population's distribution*, as long as the sample size is sufficiently large.

Student's *t*-Distribution

- Symmetrical (bell-shaped).
- Defined by single parameter, degrees of freedom (df), where df = n − 1 for hypothesis tests and confidence intervals involving a sample mean.

- Less peaked and fatter tails than a normal distribution.
- As sample size (degrees of freedom) increases, *t*-distribution approaches normal distribution.

Student's t-distribution is similar in concept to the normal distribution in that it is bell-shaped and symmetrical about its mean. The *t-distribution* is appropriate when working with small samples (n < 30) from populations with *unknown variance* and normal, or approximately normal, distributions. It may also be appropriate to use the *t*-distribution when the population variance is unknown and the sample size is large enough that the central limit theorem will assure the sampling distribution is approximately normal.

Figure 4: Student's *t*-Distribution and Degrees of Freedom

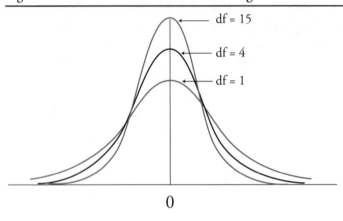

HYPOTHESIS TESTING

Hypothesis. Statement about a population parameter that is to be tested. For example, "The mean return on the S&P 500 Index is equal to zero."

Steps in Hypothesis Testing

- State the hypothesis.
- Select a test statistic.
- Specify the level of significance.
- State the decision rule for the hypothesis.
- Collect the sample and calculate statistics.
- Make a decision about the hypothesis.
- Make a decision based on the test results.

©2011 Kaplan, Inc.

Null and Alternative Hypotheses

The *null hypothesis,* designated as H_0, is the hypothesis the researcher wants to reject. It is the hypothesis that is actually tested and is the basis for the selection of the test statistics. Thus, if you believe (seek to show that) the mean return on the S&P 500 Index is different from zero, the null hypothesis will be that the mean return on the index *equals* zero.

The *alternative hypothesis,* designated H_a, is what is concluded if there is sufficient evidence to reject the null hypothesis. It is usually the alternative hypothesis you are really trying to support. Why? Because you can never really prove anything with statistics, when the null hypothesis is rejected, the implication is that the (mutually exclusive) alternative hypothesis is valid.

Two-Tailed and One-Tailed Tests

Two-tailed test. Use this type of test when testing a parameter to see if it is different from a specified value:

$H_0: \mu = 0$ versus $H_a: \mu \neq 0$

Figure 5: Two-Tailed Test: Significance = 5%, Confidence = 95%

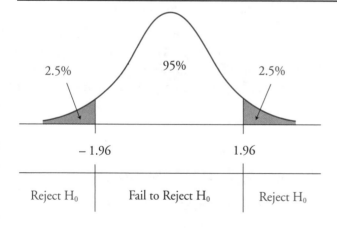

One-tailed test. Use this type of test when testing a parameter to see if it is *above* or *below* a specified value:

$H_0: \mu \leq 0$ versus $H_a: \mu > 0$, or

$H_0: \mu \geq 0$ versus $H_a: \mu < 0$

With respect to the first hypothesis, $\mu \leq 0$, we will reject it only if the test statistic is significantly greater than zero (in the right-hand tail of the distribution). Thus, we call it a one-tailed test.

Figure 6: One-Tailed Test: Significance = 5%, Confidence = 95%

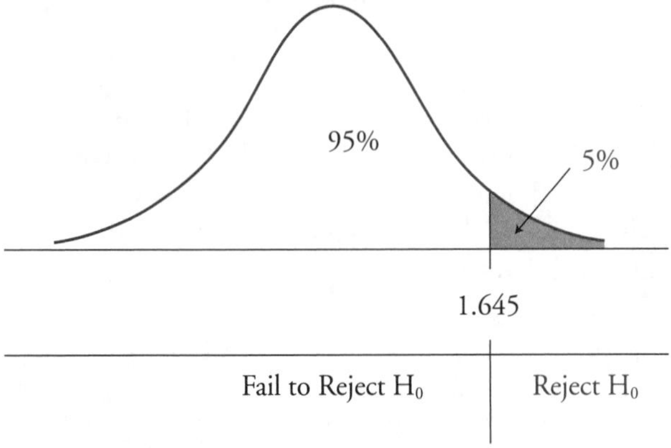

1.645

Fail to Reject H_0 Reject H_0

Test Statistic

A *test statistic* is calculated from sample data and is compared to a critical value to evaluate H_0. The most common test statistics are the z-statistic and the t-statistic. Which statistic you use to perform a hypothesis test will depend on the properties of the population and sample size, as noted previously.

- Critical values come from tables and are based on the researcher's desired level of significance. As the level of significance (α) gets smaller, the critical value gets larger and it becomes more difficult to reject the null hypothesis.
- If the test statistic exceeds the critical value (or is outside the range of critical values), the researcher rejects H_0.

Type I and Type II Errors

When testing a hypothesis, there are two possible types of errors:

1. *Type I error.* The rejection of the null hypothesis when it is actually true.

2. *Type II error.* The failure to reject the null hypothesis when it is actually false.

The *power of a test* is $1 - P(\text{Type II error})$. The more likely that a test will reject a false null, the more powerful the test. A test that is unlikely to reject a false null has little power.

Significance Level (α)

The *significance level* is the probability of making a Type I error (i.e., rejecting the null when it is true) and is designated by the Greek letter alpha (α). You can think of this as the probability that the test statistic exceeded or fell below a critical value by chance. A significance level of 5% ($\alpha = 0.05$) means there is a 5% chance of rejecting a true null hypothesis.

Figure 7: Errors in Hypothesis Testing

Type I and Type II Errors in Hypothesis Testing		
	True Condition	
Decision	H_0 is true	H_0 is false
Do not reject H_0	Correct decision	Incorrect decision Type II error
Reject H_0	Incorrect decision Type I error Significance level, α, = P(Type I error)	Correct decision Power of the test = 1 − P(Type II error)

Economics (Study Session 4)

Basic microeconomic concepts (e.g., elasticity, economic versus accounting profit, the principal-agent problem, fixed versus variable costs, and types of economic markets) and macroeconomic concepts (e.g., factors of production, business cycles, inflation, money demand, and fiscal and monetary policy) are the foundations for industry analysis, as well as equity and fixed income valuation. For example, the Porter framework depends heavily on basic microeconomic concepts.

Demand and Supply Analysis

Price Elasticity of Demand

- *Price elasticity of demand.* Refers to the change in the quantity demanded of a good in relation to the change in price. As the price of a good increases, the quantity demanded decreases.
- *Elastic demand.* A small price increase causes a large decrease in the quantity demanded.
- *Inelastic demand.* A large price increase causes a small decrease in quantity demanded.
- *Perfectly elastic demand.* A small price increase reduces the quantity demanded to zero (a horizontal demand curve).
- *Perfectly inelastic demand.* A price change does not affect the quantity demanded (a vertical demand curve).

Be familiar with the relationship between price and total revenue, based on elasticity of demand. If demand is elastic, a price decrease would lead to higher total revenue because the percentage increase in the quantity demanded is greater than the percentage decrease in price. When demand is inelastic, price and total revenue move in the same direction.

Price elasticity has two main determinants:

- *Availability of substitutes.* If good substitutes are available, consumers may switch to a substitute good if prices rise. The presence of many substitutes will tend to increase demand elasticity.
- *Share of budget spent on product.* Goods that occupy a relatively *small* portion of your budget will tend to be price *inelastic*.

Elasticity is *greater in the long run*, as consumers can make more adjustments based on the new price of the good.

Income Elasticity of Demand

Income elasticity is a similar concept that describes the sensitivity of demand to a change in consumer income (holding the price of the good constant).

An *inferior good* has negative income elasticity. As income increases (decreases), demand decreases (increases). Inferior goods include such things as bus travel and margarine.

A *normal good* has positive income elasticity; as income increases (decreases), demand for the good increases (decreases). Normal goods include things like bread and tobacco.

Cross Price Elasticity of Demand

Cross price elasticity measures the change in demand for one good in response to a change in the price of another good that is a substitute for it or a complement to it.

- If the two goods are *substitutes,* cross price elasticity is positive (e.g., ice cream and frozen yogurt).
- If the two goods are *complements,* cross price elasticity is negative (e.g., autos and gasoline).

Elasticity of Supply

Price elasticity of supply measures the responsiveness of the quantity supplied to changes in price.

Considering a linear demand curve, the elasticity will be different at different points on the curve (i.e., constant slope does not imply constant elasticity). At lower quantities (higher prices), the percentage change in quantity is relatively larger than the percentage change in price. When this is the case, demand elasticity is greater than one (in absolute value), demand is said to be elastic, and an increase in price will decrease total revenue (P × Q). At higher quantities (lower prices), the percentage change in quantity is relatively smaller than the percentage change in price. When this is the case, demand elasticity is less than one (in absolute value), demand is said to be inelastic, and an increase in price will increase total revenue (P × Q). At the point on the demand curve where total revenue (P × Q) is at a maximum, either an increase or decrease in price will decrease total revenue (demand elasticity is equal to −1 and is said to be unitary elastic or to have unitary elasticity).

Explicit vs. Implicit Costs; Economic vs. Accounting Profit

Explicit costs are the measurable costs of doing business that are reflected on a firm's accounting statement.

Implicit costs include the opportunity costs of a firm's equity and owner-provided services.

In practice, *accounting profit* only includes explicit costs and ignores implicit costs, such as the opportunity cost of equity capital.

Economic profit considers both the explicit and implicit costs. When the firm's revenues are just equal to its costs (explicit and implicit, including the normal rate of return), economic profits are zero and equity capital earns a competitive rate of return.

- *Economic costs.* Reflect explicit and implicit costs.
- *Accounting costs.* Reflect only explicit costs.

Economic Rent and Opportunity Cost

Opportunity cost of a worker is what he could earn in his next highest paying employment.

Economic rent is the difference between what a worker earns and his opportunity cost.

Short-Run and Long-Run Costs

In the *short run*, it is difficult to alter production methods. The short run is defined as that time period in which the size of plant and equipment cannot be changed. The length of the short run varies from industry to industry.

The *long run* is the period of time necessary for the firm to change its production methods, scale of operation, and resource uses. In the long run, all resources (costs) are variable.

Types of Costs

- *Fixed costs*, sometimes called *sunk costs*, remain unchanged in the short run and are therefore not considered when making short-run production decisions. They are related to the passage of time, not the level of production.

- *Average fixed costs* are total fixed costs divided by output. Average fixed costs decline as output increases.
- *Variable costs* (e.g., wages and raw materials) are incurred when the firm produces output. They are related to the level of production, not the passage of time.
- *Average variable cost* equals the total variable cost divided by output.
- *Average total cost* equals the total costs (fixed and variable) divided by the number of units produced.
- *Marginal cost* is the additional cost of producing one more unit of output.

Law of Diminishing Returns

The *law of diminishing returns* states that as more of one input (e.g., labor) is devoted to a production process, holding the quantity of other inputs constant, output increases at a decreasing rate. For example, if an acre of corn needs to be picked, the addition of a second and third worker is highly productive. But if you already have 30 workers in the field, the additional output of the 31st worker is likely less than that of the 30th worker.

DEMAND AND SUPPLY IN FACTOR MARKETS

Marginal revenue is the addition to total revenue from selling one more unit of output. *Marginal revenue product* is the addition to total revenue gained by selling the additional output from employing one more unit of a productive resource (input).

Barriers to Entry

Markets with high barriers to entry have the potential for firms to earn economic profits, even over the long run. Barriers to entry take the forms of:

- Economies of scale (very large costs to produce at the efficient scale).
- Government licensing and legal barriers.
- Patents or exclusive rights.
- Control of resources.

Monopoly vs. Oligopoly

A *monopoly* is a market structure characterized by a single firm that sells a well-defined product for which there are no good substitutes and high entry barriers. Monopolists are price searchers and can earn positive economic profits in the long run.

An *oligopoly* is characterized by a small number of firms. With an oligopoly, decisions made by one firm affect the demand, price, and profit of others in the industry.

If oligopolies could collude perfectly, they could set the same price and output as a profit-maximizing monopolist and earn the same profits. They would need to agree both on the price and how much each producer would sell, which serves to allocate the (monopoly) profits. In practice, there are many obstacles to collusion that limit firms' economic profits in an oligopoly market structure.

UNDERSTANDING BUSINESS CYCLES

A business cycle is characterized by fluctuations in economic activity and has two phases (contraction and expansion) and two turning points (trough and peak).

Key variables used to determine the phase of cycle are:

- Real GDP.
- Real income.
- Employment.
- Industrial production.
- Wholesale-retail sales.

Figure 8: Phases of the Business Cycle

Real GDP

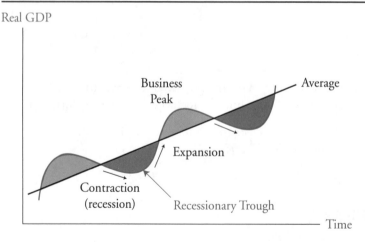

©2011 Kaplan, Inc.

Inflation

Inflation is a protracted period of rising prices. The *rate of inflation* is the rate of change in a price index over a given period of time:

$$\text{inflation rate: } i = \frac{\text{this year's price index} - \text{last year's price index}}{\text{last year's price index}}$$

The consumer price index (CPI) is the best known indicator of U.S. inflation. The CPI is believed to overstate inflation by about 1% per year because the CPI does not account for quality improvements in or substitution between goods.

FINANCIAL REPORTING AND ANALYSIS (STUDY SESSIONS 5, 6, & 7)

At Level II, you will not be directly tested on Level I financial reporting and analysis topics. However, the Level II curriculum assumes that you have retained a working knowledge of many of the Level I LOS, particularly those on the statement of cash flows, ratios, and items on income statements and balance sheets. The Level I material most directly applies to the Level II topic review on analysis of financial statements in Study Session 7, but the Level I material is interwoven into many other Level II LOS. For example, the capital budgeting material in corporate finance asks you to evaluate how the choice of depreciation method affects the cash flows for an expansion or replacement project.

We strongly recommend that anyone who struggled with financial reporting and analysis at Level I review this material before starting your Level II review. It will make things easier at Level II!

FINANCIAL STATEMENT ANALYSIS: AN INTRODUCTION

The statement of comprehensive income reports all changes in equity except for shareholder transactions. The **income statement** reports on the firm's financial performance over a period of time. The elements of the income statement include revenues, expenses, gains, and losses.

- *Revenues* are inflows from delivering or producing goods, rendering services, or other activities that constitute the entity's ongoing major or central operations.
- *Expenses* are outflows from delivering or producing goods or services that constitute the entity's ongoing major or central operations.
- *Gains and losses* are increases (decreases) in equity or net assets from peripheral or incidental transactions.

The **balance sheet** reports the firm's financial position at a point in time. The balance sheet consists of three elements:

1. *Assets* are resources obtained or controlled by a particular entity as a result of past transactions or events that are expected to provide current or future economic benefits.

2. *Liabilities* are obligations to transfer assets or provide services to other entities in the future as a result of past transactions or events.

3. *Owners' equity* is the residual interest in the assets of an entity that remains after deducting its liabilities.

Transactions are measured so that the fundamental accounting equation holds:

assets = liabilities + owners' equity

The **cash flow statement** reports the company's cash receipts and outflows. These cash flows are classified as follows:

- *Operating cash flows* include the cash effects of transactions that involve the normal business of the firm.
- *Investing cash flows* are those resulting from acquisition or sale of property, plant, and equipment, of a subsidiary or segment, and purchase or sale of investments in other firms.
- *Financing cash flows* are those resulting from issuance or retirement of debt and equity securities and dividends paid to stockholders.

The **statement of changes in equity** reports the amounts and sources of changes in equity investors' investment in the firm.

Financial statement notes (footnotes) include disclosures that offer further detail about the information summarized in the financial statements. Footnotes allow users to improve their assessments of the amount, timing, and uncertainty of the estimates reported in the financial statements. Footnotes:

- Provide information about accounting methods and the assumptions and estimates used by management.
- Are audited, whereas other disclosures, such as supplementary schedules, are not audited.
- Provide additional information on such items as fixed assets, inventory, income taxes, pensions, debt, contingencies and commitments, marketable securities, significant customers, sales to related parties, and export sales.
- Often contain disclosures relating to contingent losses.

Supplementary schedules contain additional information. Examples of such disclosures are:

- Operating income or sales by region or business segment.
- Reserves for an oil and gas company.
- Information about hedging activities and financial instruments.

Management's Commentary or **Management's Discussion and Analysis** (MD&A) provides an assessment of the financial performance and condition of a company from the perspective of its management. For publicly held companies in the United States, the MD&A is required to discuss:

- Significant events and uncertainties that affect the firm's liquidity, capital resources, and results of operations.

- Effects of inflation and changing prices if material.
- Impact of off-balance-sheet obligations and contractual obligations such as purchase commitments.
- Accounting policies that require significant judgment by management.
- Forward-looking expenditures and divestitures.

Financial Statement Elements

Financial statement elements are the major classifications of assets, liabilities, owners' equity, revenues, and expenses. **Accounts** are the specific records within each element where specific transactions are entered. **Contra accounts** are used for entries that offset other accounts.

Assets are the firm's economic resources. Examples of assets include the following:

- *Cash and cash equivalents.* Risk-free securities with original maturities of 90 days or less.
- *Accounts receivable.* Accounts receivable often have an "allowance for bad debt expense" as a contra account.
- *Inventories.*
- *Financial assets.* Includes marketable securities.
- *Prepaid expenses.* Items that will show up on future income statements as expenses.
- *Property, plant, and equipment.* Includes a contra-asset account for accumulated depreciation.
- *Investment in affiliates.* Accounted for using the equity method.
- *Deferred tax assets.*
- *Intangible assets.* Economic resources of the firm that do not have a physical form, such as patents, trademarks, licenses, and goodwill.

Liabilities are claims that creditors have on the company's resources. Examples of liabilities include the following:

- *Accounts payable* and *trade payables.*
- *Financial liabilities.* Includes short-term notes payable.
- *Unearned revenue.* Items that will show up on future income statements as revenues.
- *Income taxes payable.* The taxes accrued during the past year but not yet paid.
- *Long-term debt.* Includes bonds payable.
- *Deferred tax liabilities.*

Owners' equity is the claim that the firm's owners have on its resources, which is the amount by which assets exceed liabilities. Owners' equity includes the following:

- *Capital.* Par value of common stock.
- *Additional paid-in capital.* Proceeds from common stock sales above par value. (Share repurchases that the company has made are represented in the contra account *Treasury stock.*)
- *Retained earnings.* Cumulative income that has not been distributed as dividends.
- *Noncontrolling (minority) interest.* Minority shareholders' pro rata share of the equity of a subsidiary that is not wholly owned by the parent.
- *Other comprehensive income.* Changes in carrying amounts of assets and liabilities.

Revenue represents inflows of economic resources and includes the following:

- *Sales.* Revenue from the firm's day-to-day activities.
- *Gains.* Increases in assets or equity from transactions incidental to the firm's day-to-day activities.
- *Investment income.* Includes interest and dividend income.

Expenses are outflows of economic resources and include the following:

- *Cost of goods sold.*
- *Selling, general, and administrative expenses.* These include such expenses as advertising, salaries, rent, and utilities.
- *Depreciation* and *amortization.*
- *Tax expense.*
- *Interest expense.*
- *Losses.* Decreases in assets or equity from transactions incidental to the firm's day-to-day activities.

The Accounting Equation

The basic accounting equation (what balances in a balance sheet):

$$\text{assets} = \text{liabilities} + \text{owners' equity}$$

The expanded accounting equation shows the components of owners' equity:

$$\text{assets} = \text{liabilities} + \text{contributed capital} + \text{ending retained earnings}$$

Level I Refresher

The expanded accounting equation can also be stated as:

assets = liabilities
+ contributed capital
+ beginning retained earnings
+ revenue
− expenses
− dividends

Keeping the accounting equation in balance requires **double-entry accounting**, in which a transaction has to be recorded in at least two accounts. An increase in an asset account, for example, must be balanced by a decrease in another asset account or by an increase in a liability or owners' equity account.

Accruals and Adjustments

Revenues and expenses are not always recorded at the same time cash changes hands. The principle of **accrual accounting** requires that revenue is recorded when the firm earns it and expenses are recorded when the firm incurs them, regardless of whether cash has actually been paid. Accruals fall into four categories:

1. *Unearned revenue:* Cash increases and a liability for the goods or services the firm must provide in the future is recorded in the same amount.

2. *Accrued revenue:* Revenue is recorded for credit sales, accounts receivable increases, and inventory decreases.

3. *Prepaid expenses:* Cash decreases and an asset (prepaid expenses) increases. The asset decreases and expenses increase when the expense is actually incurred.

4. *Accrued expenses:* The firm owes cash for expenses it has incurred but has not paid. A liability for accrued expenses, such as wages payable, increases.

With unearned revenue and prepaid expenses, cash changes hands first, and the revenue or expense is recorded later. With accrued revenue and accrued expenses, the revenue or expense is recorded first. In all these cases, the effect of accrual accounting is to recognize revenues or expenses in the appropriate period.

Understanding Income Statements

Recognition of Expense

Under the accrual method of accounting, expense recognition is based on the *matching principle* whereby expenses for producing goods and services are recognized in the period in which the revenue for the goods and services is recognized. Expenses that are not tied directly to generating revenue, such as administrative costs, are called *period costs* and are expensed in the period incurred.

The cost of long-lived assets must also be matched with revenues. The allocation of cost over an asset's useful life is known as **depreciation** or **amortization** expense.

If a firm sells goods or services on credit or provides a warranty to the customer, the **matching principle** requires the firm to estimate bad-debt expense and/or warranty expense. Because estimates are involved, it is possible for firms to delay the recognition of expense. Delayed expense recognition increases net income and is, therefore, more aggressive.

Intangible Assets

Amortization expense of intangible assets with limited lives is similar to depreciation; the expense should match the benefits/value used up. Most firms, however, use the straight-line method. Goodwill and other intangible assets with indefinite lives are not amortized. However, they are tested for impairment at least annually. If the asset is impaired, an expense is recognized in the income statement.

Items Excluded From the Income Statement That Affect Owners' Equity

Transactions with owners:

1. Issuing or reacquiring stock.
2. Dividends paid.

Transactions included in other comprehensive income:

1. Foreign currency translation gains and losses.
2. Adjustments for pension liability.
3. Unrealized gains and losses from *cash flow hedging* derivatives.
4. Unrealized gains and losses from *available-for-sale* securities.

Comprehensive income is a measure that includes all changes to equity other than owner contributions and distributions.

Understanding Balance Sheets

The balance sheet shows the values of the assets and liabilities of the firm at a point in time. Values may be historical values, fair market values, or historical values adjusted for amortization of premiums or discounts. Balance sheet items can be divided into assets, liabilities, and equity.

assets = liabilities + owners' equity

Both IFRS and U.S. GAAP require firms to separately report their current assets and noncurrent assets and current and noncurrent liabilities. The current/noncurrent format is known as a **classified balance sheet** and is useful in evaluating liquidity.

Under IFRS, firms can choose to use a **liquidity-based format** if the presentation is more relevant and reliable. Liquidity-based presentations, which are often used in the banking industry, present assets and liabilities in the order of liquidity.

Accrual Process

The accrual method of accounting also creates assets and liabilities.

- Cash received in advance of recognizing revenue results in an increase in assets (cash) and an increase in liabilities (unearned revenue).
- Recognizing revenue before cash is received results in an increase in assets (accounts receivable) and an increase in equity (retained earnings). Cash paid in advance of recognizing expense results in a decrease in one asset (cash) and an increase in another asset (prepaid expenses) by the same amount.
- Recognizing an expense before cash is paid results in an increase in liabilities (accrued expenses) and a decrease in equity (retained earnings).

Current and Noncurrent Assets and Liabilities

Current assets include cash and other assets that will be converted into cash or used up within one year or operating cycle, whichever is greater.

Current liabilities are obligations that will be satisfied within one year or operating cycle, whichever is greater. More specifically, a liability that meets any of the following criteria is considered current:

- Settlement is expected during the normal operating cycle.
- It is held for trading purposes.
- Settlement is expected within one year.
- There is no unconditional right to defer settlement for at least one year.

Current assets minus current liabilities equals **working capital**.

Noncurrent assets do not meet the definition of current assets; that is, they will not be converted into cash or used up within one year or operating cycle.

Noncurrent liabilities do not meet the criteria of current liabilities.

If a firm includes (consolidates) balance sheet accounts of a subsidiary that is not 100% owned, the firm reports a **noncontrolling interest** in its consolidated balance sheet. The noncontrolling interest is the pro rata share of the subsidiary's net assets (equity) not owned by the parent company. Noncontrolling interest is reported in the equity section of the consolidated balance sheet.

Measurement Bases of Assets and Liabilities

Balance sheet assets and liabilities are valued using both **historical cost** and **fair value**.

- *Historical cost* is the value that was exchanged at the acquisition date. Historical cost is objective (highly reliable), but its relevance to an analyst declines as values change.
- *Fair value* is the amount at which an asset could be bought or sold, or a liability can be incurred or settled, between knowledgeable, willing parties in an arm's length transaction.

The financial statement footnotes should include the following information about the measurement of its assets and liabilities:

- Basis for measurement.
- Carrying value of inventory by category.
- Amount of inventory carried at fair value less costs to sell.
- Write-downs and reversals, with a discussion of the circumstances that led to the reversal.
- Inventories pledged as collateral for liabilities.
- Inventories recognized as an expense.

Some of the more common **current assets** are:

- **Cash and cash equivalents**—unless restrictions prohibit the use of these assets for more than 12 months, cash equivalents typically mature in 90 days or less (e.g., 90-day T-bills).
- **Accounts receivable (trade receivables)**—amounts expected to be collected from the sale of goods and services. Receivables are reported net of any allowance for bad debt.

- **Inventories**—items held for sale or used in the manufacture of goods to be sold. Manufacturing firms separately report raw materials, work-in-process, and finished goods inventories.
- **Marketable securities**—debt or equity securities that are traded in a public market (e.g., Treasury securities, certain equity securities, mutual funds).
- **Other current assets**—including prepaid expenses.

Standard costing and the retail method are used by some firms to measure inventory. **Standard costing** (often used by manufacturing firms) involves assigning predetermined costs to goods produced. Firms that use the **retail method** measure inventory at retail prices and then subtract gross profit in order to reflect cost.

Prepaid expenses are operating costs that have been paid in advance such as rent payments or insurance premiums.

Some examples of **current liabilities** are:

- **Accounts payable (trade payables)**—amounts owed to suppliers for goods or services purchased on credit.
- **Notes payable**—obligations in the form of promissory notes owed to creditors. Notes payable can also be included in noncurrent liabilities, depending on the maturity date (e.g., matures after one year or operating cycle, whichever is greater).
- **Current portion of long-term debt**—the principal portion of debt due within one year or operating cycle, whichever is greater.
- **Taxes payable**—current taxes that have been recognized in the income statement but have not yet been paid.
- **Accrued liabilities (accrued expenses)**—expenses that have been recognized in the income statement but are not yet contractually due.
- **Unearned revenue (income)**—cash collected in advance of providing goods and services. The related liability is to provide those goods and services.

Tangible Assets

Long-term assets with physical substance are known as *tangible assets*. Tangible assets, such as plant, equipment, and natural resources, are reported on the balance sheet at historical cost less accumulated depreciation or depletion.

Land is also a tangible asset that is reported at historical cost and is not depreciated.

Tangible assets not used in the operations of the firm should be classified as investment assets.

Intangible Assets

Intangible assets are long-term assets that lack physical substance. The cost of an identifiable intangible asset is amortized over its useful life. Examples of identifiable intangible assets include patents, trademarks, and copyrights.

An intangible asset that is *unidentifiable* cannot be purchased separately and may have an infinite life. The best example of an unidentifiable intangible asset is goodwill.

Goodwill is created when a business is purchased for more than the fair value of its assets net of liabilities. Goodwill is not amortized but must be tested for impairment (i.e., a decrease in its fair value) at least annually. Because goodwill is not amortized, firms can manipulate net income upward by allocating more of the acquisition price to goodwill and less to the identifiable assets. The result is less depreciation and amortization expense and thus higher net income.

When computing ratios, analysts should eliminate goodwill from the balance sheet and goodwill impairment charges from the income statement for comparability. Also, analysts should evaluate future acquisitions in terms of the price paid relative to the earning power of the acquired firm.

Intangible assets that are purchased are reported on the balance sheet at historical cost less accumulated amortization. Except for certain legal costs, intangible assets that are created internally, including research and development costs, are expensed as incurred under U.S. GAAP and not shown on the balance sheet.

Under IFRS, a firm must identify the research stage and the development stage. Accordingly, the firm must expense costs during the research stage but *may* capitalize costs incurred during the development stage.

All of the following should be expensed as incurred, rather than creating balance sheet assets:

- Start-up and training costs.
- Administrative overhead.
- Advertising and promotion costs.
- Relocation and reorganization costs.
- Termination costs.

Some analysts completely eliminate intangible assets, particularly unidentifiable intangibles, for analytical purposes. This is inadvisable. Analysts should consider the economic value of each intangible asset before making an adjustment.

Components of Owners' Equity

Owners' equity is the residual interest in assets that remains after subtracting an entity's liabilities. The owners' equity section of the balance sheet includes:

- **Contributed capital**—the total amount received from the issuance of common and preferred stock. The par value of common stock and preferred stock is a "stated" or "legal" value. The amounts paid over par value are recorded as "paid-in-capital in excess of par value."
- **Noncontrolling interest** (minority interest)—the minority shareholders' pro rata share of the net assets (equity) of a consolidated subsidiary that is not wholly owned by the parent.
- **Retained earnings**—the undistributed earnings (net income) of the firm since inception; that is, the cumulative earnings that have not been paid out to shareholders as dividends.
- **Treasury stock**—stock that has been reacquired by the issuing firm but not yet retired. Treasury stock reduces stockholders' equity; it does not represent an investment in the firm. Treasury stock has no voting rights and does not receive dividends.
- **Accumulated other comprehensive income**—includes all changes in stockholders' equity except for transactions recognized in the income statement and transactions with shareholders such as issuing stock, reacquiring stock, and paying dividends.

The **statement of changes in equity** summarizes all transactions that increase or decrease the equity accounts for the period. The statement includes transactions with shareholders (e.g., issuance or repurchase of stock) and a reconciliation of the beginning and ending balances of each equity account including capital stock, additional paid-in-capital, retained earnings, and accumulated other comprehensive income. In addition, the components of accumulated other comprehensive income are disclosed (e.g., unrealized gains and losses from available-for-sale securities, cash flow hedging derivatives, foreign currency translation, and adjustments for minimum pension liability).

UNDERSTANDING CASH FLOW STATEMENTS

The **cash flow statement** provides information beyond that available from net income and other financial data. The cash flow statement provides information about a firm's liquidity, solvency, and financial flexibility. The cash flow statement reconciles the beginning and ending balances of cash over an accounting period. The change in cash is a result of the firm's operating, investing, and financing activities as follows:

	operating activities
+	investing activities
+	financing activities
=	change in cash balance
+	beginning cash balance
=	ending cash balance

Figure 9: U.S. GAAP Cash Flow Classifications

Operating Activities

Inflows	*Outflows*
Cash collected from customers	Cash paid to employees and suppliers
Interest and dividends received	Cash paid for other expenses
Sale proceeds from trading securities	Acquisition of trading securities
	Interest paid
	Taxes paid

Investing Activities

Inflows	*Outflows*
Sale proceeds from fixed assets	Acquisition of fixed assets
Sale proceeds from debt & equity investments	Acquisition of debt & equity investments
Principal received from loans made to others	Loans made to others

Financing Activities

Inflows	*Outflows*
Principal amounts borrowed from others	Principal paid on amounts from others
Proceeds from issuing stock	Payments to reacquire stock
	Dividends paid to shareholders

Differences Between U.S. GAAP and IFRS

Under IFRS:

- Interest and dividends received may be classified as either CFO or CFI.
- Dividends paid to shareholders and interest paid on debt may be classified as either CFO or CFF.
- Income taxes are reported as operating activities unless the expense can be tied to an investing or financing transaction.

Noncash investing and financing activities are not reported in the cash flow statement but must be disclosed in either a footnote or a supplemental schedule to the cash flow statement.

Direct Method and Indirect Methods Calculating CFO

There are two different methods of presenting the cash flow statement permitted under U.S. GAAP and IFRS—the direct method and the indirect method. The use of the direct method is encouraged by both standard setters. The difference in the two methods relates to the presentation of cash flow from operating activities. Total cash flow from operating activities is exactly the same under both methods, and the presentation of cash flow from investing activities and from financing activities is exactly the same under both methods.

The direct method provides more information than the indirect method. The main advantage of the indirect method is that it focuses on the differences between net income and operating cash flow.

Direct Method

The direct method presents operating cash flow by taking each item from the income statement and converting it to its cash equivalent by adding or subtracting the changes in the corresponding balance sheet accounts. The following are examples of operating cash flow components:

- Cash collected from sales is the main component of CFO. Cash collections are calculated by adjusting sales for the changes in accounts receivable and unearned (deferred) revenue.
- Cash used in the production of goods and services (cash inputs) is calculated by adjusting cost of goods sold (COGS) for the changes in inventory and accounts payable.

Indirect Method

Using the indirect method, operating cash flow is calculated in four steps:

Step 1: Begin with net income.

Step 2: Subtract gains or add losses that resulted from financing or investing cash flows (e.g., gains from sale of land).

Step 3: Add back all noncash charges to income (e.g., depreciation and amortization) and subtract all noncash components of revenue.

Step 4: Add or subtract changes to related balance sheet operating accounts as follows:

- Increases in the operating asset accounts (uses of cash) are subtracted, while decreases (sources of cash) are added.
- Increases in the operating liability accounts (sources of cash) are added, while decreases (uses of cash) are subtracted.

Most firms present the cash flow statement using the indirect method. For analytical purposes, it may be beneficial to *convert the cash flow statement to the direct method.* Examples of such conversion for two items are:

- Cash collections from customers:
  1. Begin with net sales from the income statement.
  2. Subtract (add) any increase (decrease) in the accounts receivable balance as reported in the indirect method.
  3. Add (subtract) an increase (decrease) in unearned revenue.

- Cash payments to suppliers:
  1. Begin with cost of goods sold (COGS) as reported in the income statement.
  2. If depreciation and/or amortization have been included in COGS (they increase COGS), they must be eliminated when computing the cash paid to suppliers.
  3. Subtract (add) any increase (decrease) in the accounts payable balance as reported in the indirect method.
  4. Add (subtract) any increase (decrease) in the inventory balance as disclosed in the indirect method.
  5. Subtract any inventory write-off that occurred during the period.

Analysis of the Cash Flow Statement

1. **Operating Cash Flow**

   The analyst should identify the major determinants of operating cash flow. Positive operating cash flow can be generated by the firm's earning-related activities. However, positive operating cash flow can also be generated by decreasing noncash working capital, such as liquidating inventory, reducing receivables, or increasing payables. Decreasing noncash working capital is not sustainable, because inventories and receivables cannot fall below zero and creditors will not extend credit indefinitely unless payments are made.

Operating cash flow also provides a check of the quality of a firm's earnings. A stable relationship of operating cash flow and net income is an indication of quality earnings but is affected by the stage of business cycle and the firm's life cycle. Earnings that exceed operating cash flow may be an indication of aggressive accounting choices such as premature recognition of revenues or delayed recognition of expenses. The variability of net income and operating cash flow should also be considered.

2. **Investing Cash Flow**

   Increasing capital expenditures, a use of cash, is usually an indication of growth. Conversely, a firm may reduce capital expenditures or even sell capital assets in order to save or generate cash. This may result in higher cash outflows in the future as older assets are replaced or growth resumes.

3. **Financing Cash Flow**

   The financing activities section of the cash flow statement reveals information about whether the firm is generating cash by issuing debt or equity. It also provides information about whether the firm is using cash to repay debt, reacquire stock, or pay dividends.

The cash flow statement can be converted to **common-size format** by expressing each line item as a percentage of revenue. Alternatively, each inflow of cash can be expressed as a percentage of total cash inflows and each outflow of cash can be expressed as a percentage of total cash outflows.

Free cash flow is a measure of cash that is available for discretionary purposes, that is, the cash flow that is available once the firm has covered its obligations and capital expenditures.

Free cash flow to the firm (FCFF) is the cash available to all investors, including stockholders and debtholders.

Free cash flow to equity (FCFE) is the cash flow that is available for distribution to the common shareholders, that is, after all obligations have been paid.

ANALYSIS OF FINANCIAL STATEMENTS: RATIOS

With respect to analysis of financial statements, there are a number of key ratios, including the following:

- Current, quick, and cash ratios.
- All the ratios in the cash conversion cycle (the turnover ratios are more important, like receivables, inventory, and payables turnover).
- Turnover ratios use sales in the numerator, except for payables and inventory turnover ratios, which use COGS.
- Gross profit margin, net profit margin, and operating profit margin are readily available from a common-size income statement.
- Return on equity (ROE) is critical. Definitely know the three- and five-component DuPont ROE decompositions.
- Debt-to-equity, total debt, interest coverage, and fixed financial coverage ratios (remember to add lease interest expense to numerator *and* denominator).
- The retention ratio and *g*.

Common-size balance sheets and income statements. These statements normalize balance sheets and income statements and allow the analyst to make easier comparisons of different-sized firms. A common-size balance sheet expresses all balance sheet accounts as a *percentage of total assets*. A common-size income statement expresses all income statement items as a *percentage of sales*.

Measures of liquidity:

$$\text{current ratio} = \frac{\text{current assets}}{\text{current liabilities}}$$

$$\text{quick ratio} = \frac{\text{cash} + \text{marketable securities} + \text{receivables}}{\text{current liabilities}}$$

Turnover ratios and the cash conversion cycle:

$$\text{receivables turnover} = \frac{\text{net annual sales}}{\text{average receivables}}$$

$$\text{inventory turnover} = \frac{\text{cost of goods sold}}{\text{average inventory}}$$

$$\text{payables turnover ratio} = \frac{\text{purchases}}{\text{average trade payables}}$$

$$\text{average receivables collection period} = \frac{365}{\text{receivables turnover}}$$

$$\text{average inventory processing period} = \frac{365}{\text{inventory turnover}}$$

$$\text{payables payment period} = \frac{365}{\text{payables turnover ratio}}$$

$$\begin{array}{l}\text{cash} \\ \text{conversion} \\ \text{cycle}\end{array} = \begin{pmatrix}\text{average receivables} \\ \text{collection period}\end{pmatrix} + \begin{pmatrix}\text{average inventory} \\ \text{processing period}\end{pmatrix} - \begin{pmatrix}\text{payables} \\ \text{payment} \\ \text{period}\end{pmatrix}$$

Measures of operating performance—operating efficiency ratios: total asset, fixed-asset, and equity turnover.

$$\text{total asset turnover} = \frac{\text{net sales}}{\text{average total net assets}}$$

$$\text{fixed asset turnover} = \frac{\text{net sales}}{\text{average net fixed assets}}$$

$$\text{equity turnover} = \frac{\text{net sales}}{\text{average equity}}$$

Measures of operating performance—operating profitability ratios: gross, operating, and net profit margins.

$$\text{gross profit margin} = \frac{\text{gross profit}}{\text{net sales}}$$

$$\text{operating profit margin} = \frac{\text{operating profit}}{\text{net sales}} = \frac{\text{EBIT}}{\text{net sales}}$$

$$\text{net profit margin} = \frac{\text{net income}}{\text{net sales}}$$

Return on total capital (ROTC):

$$\text{return on total capital} = \frac{\text{net income} + \text{interest expense}}{\text{average total capital}}$$

Total capital includes debt capital, so interest is added back to net income.

Return on equity (ROE):

$$\text{return on total equity} = \frac{\text{net income}}{\text{average total equity}}$$

$$\text{return on common equity} = \frac{\text{net income} - \text{preferred dividends}}{\text{average common equity}}$$

Measures of financial risk: debt-equity ratio and the total debt ratio.

$$\text{debt-equity ratio} = \frac{\text{total long-term debt}}{\text{total equity}}$$

$$\text{total debt ratio} = \frac{\text{current liabilities} + \text{total long-term debt}}{\text{total debt} + \text{total equity}}$$

Interest coverage: cash flow to long-term debt ratio.

$$\text{interest coverage} = \frac{\text{EBIT}}{\text{interest expense}}$$

$$\frac{\text{cash flow to}}{\text{long-term debt}} = \frac{\text{CFO}}{\text{book value of long-term debt} + \text{PV of operating leases}}$$

Growth analysis:

$$g = \text{retention rate} \times \text{ROE}$$

$$\text{retention rate} = 1 - \frac{\text{dividends declared}}{\text{operating income after taxes}}$$

DuPont analysis. The DuPont method is used to decompose ROE in order to better analyze firm performance. An analyst can see the impact of leverage, profit margin, and turnover on ROE. There are two variants of the DuPont system: the traditional approach and the extended system.

Level I Refresher

Both approaches begin with:

$$\text{return on equity} = \left(\frac{\text{net income}}{\text{equity}}\right)$$

The *traditional DuPont equation* is:

$$\text{return on equity} = \left(\frac{\text{net income}}{\text{sales}}\right)\left(\frac{\text{sales}}{\text{assets}}\right)\left(\frac{\text{assets}}{\text{equity}}\right)$$

You may also see it presented as:

$$\text{return on equity} = \left(\begin{array}{c}\text{net profit} \\ \text{margin}\end{array}\right)\left(\begin{array}{c}\text{asset} \\ \text{turnover}\end{array}\right)\left(\begin{array}{c}\text{equity} \\ \text{multiplier}\end{array}\right)$$

The *traditional DuPont equation* is arguably the most important equation in ratio analysis because it breaks down a very important ratio (ROE) into three key components. If ROE is low, it must be that at least one of the following is true: the company has a poor profit margin, the company has poor asset turnover, or the firm is under-leveraged.

The *extended DuPont equation* takes the net profit margin and breaks it down further. The extended DuPont equation can be written as:

$$\text{ROE} = \left(\frac{\text{net income}}{\text{EBT}}\right)\left(\frac{\text{EBT}}{\text{EBIT}}\right)\left(\frac{\text{EBIT}}{\text{revenue}}\right)\left(\frac{\text{revenue}}{\text{total assets}}\right)\left(\frac{\text{total assets}}{\text{total equity}}\right)$$

You may also see it presented as:

$$\text{ROE} = \left(\begin{array}{c}\text{tax} \\ \text{burden}\end{array}\right)\left(\begin{array}{c}\text{interest} \\ \text{burden}\end{array}\right)\left(\begin{array}{c}\text{EBIT} \\ \text{margin}\end{array}\right)\left(\begin{array}{c}\text{asset} \\ \text{turnover}\end{array}\right)\left(\begin{array}{c}\text{financial} \\ \text{leverage}\end{array}\right)$$

Usefulness and Limitations of Ratio Analysis

Financial ratios provide useful information to analysts, including:

- Insights into the financial relationships that are useful in forecasting future earnings and cash flows.
- Information about the financial flexibility of the firm.
- A means of evaluating management's performance.

Financial ratios have limitations:

- Ratios are not useful when viewed in isolation.
- Comparisons with other companies are made more difficult because of different accounting methods. Some of the more common differences include inventory methods (FIFO and LIFO), depreciation methods (accelerated and straight-line), and lease accounting (capital and operating).
- There may be difficulty in locating comparable ratios when analyzing companies that operate in multiple industries.
- Conclusions cannot be made from viewing one set of ratios. Ratios must be viewed relative to one another.
- Judgment is required. Determining the target or comparison value for a ratio is difficult and may require some range of acceptable values.

ANALYSIS OF INCOME TAXES

From the tax return we will find:

- *Taxable income.* Represents income subject to tax as reported on the tax return.
- *Taxes payable.* Represents the tax liability based on taxable income, as shown on the tax return.
- *Income tax paid.* Actual cash outflow for taxes paid during the current period.
- *Tax loss carryforwards.* Losses that could not be deducted on the tax return in the current period but may be used to reduce taxable income and taxes payable in future periods.

On the financial statements, we find *pretax income*, which is income before income tax expense. Pretax income on the income statement is used to calculate:

- *Income tax expense.* A noncash income statement item that includes cash tax expense plus any increase in the deferred tax liability minus any increase in the deferred tax asset.
- *Deferred income tax expense.* The excess of income tax expense over taxes payable.

Deferred Tax Liabilities

Deferred tax liabilities are balance sheet amounts that result from an excess of income tax expense over taxes payable that are expected to result in future cash outflows.

The most common reason for creation of a deferred tax liability is that depreciation expense on the income statement (straight-line) is less than depreciation expense on the tax return (accelerated). Pretax income is therefore greater than taxable income, and income tax expense is greater than income tax payable. The taxes that are deferred by using accelerated depreciation on the tax return are carried as a deferred tax liability on the balance sheet.

Deferred Tax Assets

Deferred tax assets are balance sheet amounts that result when taxes payable are greater than income tax expense.

An example of this situation is warranty expense. On the income statement, estimated warranty expense is deductible; on the tax return, only warranty expense actually incurred is deductible. Early on, this leads to taxes payable being greater than income tax expense, which gives rise to a deferred tax asset. In future periods, taxes payable will be less than income tax expense, and the benefit of the asset will be realized.

Calculating deferred tax liabilities and assets. Under the *liability method*, all temporary differences between taxable income and pretax income are multiplied by the expected future tax rate (typically the current rate) to calculate deferred tax assets and liabilities. They are not netted; deferred tax assets and liabilities can be on the balance sheet simultaneously and separately.

Change in tax rates. A change in tax rates will be reflected by an adjustment to both deferred tax asset and liability accounts. A decrease (increase) in the tax rate will decrease (increase) both deferred tax assets and liabilities; the net change is reflected in income tax expense for the current period.

Financial analysis. If a company's assets are growing, it may be the case that a deferred tax liability is not expected to reverse in the foreseeable future; an analyst should treat this liability as additional equity. If the liability is expected to reverse, the liability should be adjusted to present value terms to the extent practicable. Decide which is more appropriate on a case-by-case basis.

Permanent differences. So far, our examples have been temporary differences between taxable income and pretax income that will potentially reverse over time. In the case of interest income on tax-exempt bonds, for example, pretax income is greater than taxable income, and this will not reverse. There is no deferred asset or liability created, and the tax rate on the financial statements is adjusted so taxes payable and income tax expense are equal.

IFRS AND GAAP

IFRS Treatments of Assets and Liabilities

Inventory

- Under IFRS, the choice of inventory method is based on the physical flow of the inventory. Two acceptable methods are the first-in, first-out (FIFO) method and the average cost method. The last-in, first-out (LIFO) method is allowed under U.S. GAAP but is not permitted under IFRS.
- Under both IFRS and U.S. GAAP, inventory is reported on the balance sheet at the lower of cost or net realizable value. In the United States, once an inventory write-down occurs, any subsequent recovery of value is ignored. Under IFRS, recovery of value is permitted.

Property and Equipment

- Under both IFRS and U.S. GAAP, long-term (fixed) assets are reported on the balance sheet at original cost less accumulated depreciation.
- Under IFRS, property and equipment can be revalued upward, but this is not permitted under U.S. GAAP. The increase in value is reported in the income statement to the extent that a previous downward valuation was included in net income. Otherwise, the increase in value is reported as a direct adjustment to equity.

Intercorporate Investments

Figure 10: IFRS Accounting Treatment for Intercorporate Investments

Method	Ownership	Degree of Influence
Market	Less than 20%	No significant influence
Equity	20–50%	Significant influence
Consolidation	More than 50%	Control
Proportionate Consolidation (IFRS only)	Shared	Joint control

- In the case of joint control of an investee, such as an ownership interest in a joint venture, IFRS recommends the use of the **proportionate consolidation** method, although the equity method is permitted. Under proportionate consolidation, the investor reports its pro rata share of the assets, liabilities, and net income of the investee.
- Under U.S. GAAP, the equity method is usually required for joint ventures. Proportionate consolidation is not permitted.

Goodwill

- Under IFRS No. 3, goodwill is not systematically amortized in the income statement; however, it must be tested at least annually for impairment.
- Judgment is involved in determining whether goodwill is impaired, so the timing of impairment charges can be used to manage earnings.

For comparability purposes, analysts often make the following adjustments when performing financial analysis:

- Deduct goodwill when computing ratios.
- Exclude goodwill impairment charges from the income statement when analyzing trends.
- Evaluate acquisitions in terms of the price paid relative to the earning power of the acquired assets.

Two other issues affect the comparability of the acquiring firm's financial statements in a business acquisition.

1. The assets and liabilities of the acquired firm are recorded at fair value at the date of acquisition. As a result, the acquiring firm reports assets and liabilities with a mixture of bases for valuation; the acquiring firm's old assets continue to be reported at historical cost while the acquired assets are booked at fair value.

2. The revenues and expenses of the acquired firm are included in the acquiring firm's income statement from the acquisition date. There is no restatement of the prior-period income statements, so the acquisition may create the illusion of growth.

Identifiable Intangible Assets

- Under U.S. GAAP and IFRS, acquired intangible assets are reported on the balance sheet at acquisition cost less accumulated amortization. The costs of internally developed intangibles are generally expensed as incurred. U.S. GAAP does not permit upward revaluations of intangible assets.
- As with property and equipment, IFRS allows upward revaluations of identifiable intangible assets. In this case, the intangible assets are reported at fair value at the revaluation date less the accumulated amortization since revaluation.
- As with property and equipment, any increase in value is reported in the income statement to the extent that a previous downward valuation was included in net income. Any increase in value beyond that is reported as a direct adjustment to equity.

Analysts must be aware that not all intangible assets are reported on the balance sheet. Some intangibles are expensed as incurred. These unrecorded assets must still be considered when valuing a firm.

CORPORATE FINANCE (STUDY SESSIONS 8 & 9)

The Level II corporate finance curriculum assumes you remember the basics of capital budgeting and the cost of capital and then builds on that knowledge. At Level II, you are still responsible for material such as computing the yearly cash flows of an expansion or a replacement capital project and calculating the discount rate for capital projects.

Level II equity requires you to build on Level I knowledge of the weighted average cost of capital (WACC) and the various approaches to calculating the cost of equity capital, including the bond yield plus risk premium approach.

MEASURES OF LEVERAGE

The **degree of operating leverage** (DOL) is defined as the percentage change in operating income (EBIT) that results from a given percentage change in sales:

$$DOL = \frac{\text{percentage change in EBIT}}{\text{percentage change in sales}} = \frac{\dfrac{\Delta EBIT}{EBIT}}{\dfrac{\Delta Q}{Q}}$$

To calculate a firm's DOL for a particular level of unit sales, Q, DOL is:

$$DOL = \frac{Q(P-V)}{Q(P-V)-F}$$

where:
Q = quantity of units sold
P = price per unit
V = variable cost per unit
F = fixed costs

The **degree of financial leverage** (DFL) is interpreted as the ratio of the percentage change in net income (or EPS) to the percentage change in EBIT.

$$DFL = \frac{\text{percentage change in EPS}}{\text{percentage change in EBIT}}$$

For a particular level of operating earnings, DFL is calculated as:

$$DFL = \frac{EBIT}{EBIT - interest}$$

SHARE REPURCHASES

A **share repurchase** will reduce the number of shares outstanding, which will tend to increase earnings per share. On the other hand, purchasing shares with company funds will reduce interest income and earnings, and purchasing shares with borrowed funds incurs interest costs, which will reduce earnings directly by the after-tax cost of the borrowed funds. The relation of the percentage decrease in earnings and the percentage decrease in the number of shares used to calculate EPS will determine whether the effect of a stock repurchase on EPS will be positive or negative.

CAPITAL BUDGETING

Capital budgeting is identifying and evaluating projects for which the cash flows extend over a period longer than a year. The process has four steps:

Step 1: Generating ideas.
Step 2: Analyzing project proposals.
Step 3: Creating the firm's capital budget.
Step 4: Monitoring decisions and conducting a post-audit.

Categories of capital budgeting projects include:

*   Replacement projects to maintain the business.
*   Replacement projects to reduce costs.
*   Expansion projects to increase capacity.
*   New product or market development.
*   Mandatory projects, such as meeting safety or environmental regulations.
*   Other projects, including high-risk research and development or management pet projects, are not easily analyzed through the capital budgeting process.

Five Key Principles of Capital Budgeting

1. Decisions are based on *incremental cash flows*. Sunk costs are not considered. Externalities, including *cannibalization* of sales from the firm's current products, should be included in the analysis.
2. Cash flows are based on *opportunity costs,* which are the cash flows the firm will lose by undertaking the project.
3. *Timing* of the cash flows is important.

4. Cash flows are analyzed on an *after-tax basis.*
5. *Financing costs* are reflected in the required rate of return on the project, *not* in the incremental cash flows.

Projects can be *independent* and evaluated separately, or *mutually exclusive,* which means the projects compete with each other and the firm can accept only one of them. In some cases, *project sequencing* requires projects to be undertaken in a certain order, with the accept/reject decision on the second project depending on the profitability of the first project.

A firm with *unlimited funds* can accept all profitable projects. However, when *capital rationing* is necessary, the firm must select the most valuable group of projects that can be funded with the limited capital resources available.

Capital Budgeting Methods

Net present value (NPV) for a normal project is the present value of all the expected future cash flows minus the initial cost of the project, using the project's cost of capital. A project that has a positive net present value should be accepted because it is expected to increase the value of the firm (shareholder wealth).

The *internal rate of return* (IRR) is the discount rate that makes the present value of the expected future cash flows equal to the initial cost of the project. If the IRR is greater than the project's cost of capital, it should be accepted because it is expected to increase firm value. If the IRR is equal to the project's cost of capital, the NPV is zero.

For an independent project, the criteria for acceptance (NPV > 0 and IRR > project cost of capital) are equivalent and always lead to the same decision.

For mutually exclusive projects, the NPV and IRR decision rules can lead to different rankings because of differences in project size and/or differences in the timing of cash flows. The NPV criterion is theoretically preferred, as it directly estimates the effect of project acceptance on firm value.

Because inflation is reflected in the WACC (or project cost of capital) calculation, future cash flows must be adjusted upward to reflect positive expected inflation, or some wealth-increasing (positive NPV) projects will be rejected.

Larger firms, public companies, and firms where management has a higher level of education tend to use NPV and IRR analysis. Private companies and European firms tend to rely more on the payback period in capital budgeting decisions.

In theory, a positive NPV project should increase the company's stock price by the project's NPV per share. In reality, stock prices reflect investor expectations about a firm's ability to identify and execute positive NPV projects in the future.

COST OF CAPITAL

Knowing how to calculate the *weighted average cost of capital* (WACC) and all of its components is critical.

$$WACC = (w_d)[k_d(1-t)] + (w_{ps})(k_{ps}) + (w_{ce})(k_{ce})$$

Where the *w*'s are the proportions of each type of capital, the *k*'s are the current costs of each type of capital (debt, preferred stock, and common stock), and *t* is the firm's *marginal* tax rate.

The proportions used for the three types of capital are target proportions and are calculated using market values. The WACC is used to compare the after-tax cost of raising capital to the expected after-tax returns on capital investments.

Cost of equity capital. There are three methods. You will likely know which to use by the information given in the problem.

1. CAPM approach: $k_{ce} = RFR + \beta(R_{market} - RFR)$
2. Discounted cash flow approach: $k_{ce} = (D_1 / P_0) + g$
3. Bond yield plus risk premium approach:
   k_{ce} = current market yield on the firm's long-term debt + risk premium

Cost of preferred stock is always calculated as follows:

$$k_{ps} = \frac{D_{ps}}{P}$$

Cost of debt is the average market yield on the firm's outstanding debt issues. Because interest is tax deductible, k_d is multiplied by $(1 - t)$.

Firm decisions about which projects to undertake are independent of the decision of how to finance firm assets at minimum cost. The firm will have long-run target weights for the percentages of common equity, preferred stock, and debt used to fund the firm. Investment decisions are based on a WACC that reflects each source of capital at its target weight, regardless of how a particular project will be financed or which capital source was most recently employed.

An analyst calculating a firm's WACC should use the firm's target capital structure if known or use the firm's current capital structure based on market values as the best indicator of its target capital structure. The analyst can incorporate trends in the company's capital structure into his estimate of the target structure. An alternative would be to apply the industry average capital structure to the firm.

A firm's WACC can increase as it raises larger amounts of capital, which means the firm has an upward-sloping *marginal cost of capital curve*. If the firm ranks its potential projects in descending IRR order, the result is a downward-sloping *investment opportunity schedule*. The amount of the capital investment required to fund all projects for which the IRR is greater than the marginal cost of capital is the firm's *optimal capital budget*.

EQUITY INVESTMENTS (STUDY SESSIONS 10, 11, & 12)

Many of the Level I equity topics carry over to and serve as a base for the Level II curriculum. You will draw on your knowledge of the organization and functioning of securities markets and industry analysis, including the business cycle. Level II also expands on Porter's five forces and competitive strategy. The main focus of the Level II equity curriculum is on valuation models. You will need to know the dividend discount model (DDM) as a baseline for using free cash flow and residual income valuation models.

ORGANIZATION AND FUNCTIONING OF SECURITIES MARKETS

Terminology of Markets

Primary markets. Sale of *new* security issues.

Secondary financial markets. Securities trade here after their initial offerings. Secondary markets provide valuable information about security values and provide liquidity for buyers of securities in the primary markets.

Secondary markets for bonds are almost entirely OTC/dealer markets.

Major banks and investment firms are dealers for municipal bonds and U.S. agency securities. Some corporates are traded on exchanges, but the great majority of them are traded by dealers in the OTC market.

Call markets. Stock is only traded at specific times. Trade bids and asks are accumulated, and one price is set that clears the market for the stock.

Continuous markets. Trades occur at any time the market is open. Price is set by either the auction process or by dealer bid-ask quotes.

Types of Orders

- *Market orders.* Immediate execution.
- *Limit orders.* Minimum selling or maximum purchase price.
- *Short sale orders.* Securities are borrowed, sold, and later returned.
- *Stop loss orders.* Sell orders below market price to protect long positions and buy orders above market price to protect short positions.

Short Sales

Short sales are orders to sell securities the seller does not own. For a short sale, the short seller (1) simultaneously borrows and sells securities through a broker, (2) must return the securities at the request of the lender or when the short sale is closed out, (3) must post margin and keep proceeds of the short sale on deposit with the broker, and (4) must *pay all dividends due* to the lender of the security.

ALTERNATIVE INVESTMENTS (STUDY SESSION 13)

REAL ESTATE INVESTMENTS

> The Level II LOS do not directly use formulas and concepts from Level I, so don't necessarily memorize the formulas that follow. We included them as review material. Instead, review this material quickly and then concentrate on what is required in the Level II LOS.

Types of Real Estate Investments

- *Outright ownership.*
- *Leveraged equity position.*
- *Mortgages.*
- *Aggregation vehicles.* Common forms include real estate limited partnerships, commingled funds, and real estate investment trusts (REITs).

Characteristics of Real Estate Investments

Because each property is unique, it is impossible to directly compare to other properties, making it difficult to determine true market value. Real estate as an asset class is somewhat illiquid because it is immobile, indivisible, and difficult to value.

Common methods to value real estate:

- The *cost method* is determined by the replacement cost of improvements, plus an estimate for the value of the land. The market value of an existing property may differ significantly from its replacement cost.
- The *sales comparison method* uses the price of a similar property or properties from recent transactions. Prices from other properties must be adjusted for changes in market conditions and for characteristics unique to each property. In *hedonic* price estimation, sales prices are regressed on key characteristics related to value, and then the model coefficients are used with characteristic values for the subject property to estimate its value.
- The *income method* uses the discounted annual cash flow as if it were a perpetuity to calculate the present value of the future income stream produced by the property. The net operating income (NOI) is a simplified estimate of annual cash flow equal to annual potential gross rental income minus operating expenses, which include an estimate of the percentage losses from vacancy and collection losses. The NOI is then divided by an estimate

of the market's required rate of return on similar properties, resulting in an appraisal price.

This simplified model is used quite frequently:

$$NOI = \text{potential income } (1 - \text{vacancy and bad debt \%})$$
$$- \text{RE taxes} - \text{maintenance} - \text{other expenses}$$

$$\text{real estate value (income method)} = \frac{NOI}{\text{required return}}$$

- The *discounted after-tax cash flow model* is based on the cash flows to a specific investor and, therefore, depends on the investor's marginal tax rate and the assumed financing for the transaction. The net present value of the property is calculated as the present value of the annual after-tax cash flows, discounted at the investor's required rate of return, minus the initial cash investment. In calculating the annual after-tax operating cash flows, note that interest is tax deductible and principal repayments are not.

$$\text{annual after-tax operating cash flow} = (NOI - \text{depreciation} - \text{interest})$$
$$\times (1 - \text{tax rate}) - \text{principal repayment}$$
$$+ \text{depreciation}$$

In the year of sale, the after-tax proceeds of the sale are added to that year's after-tax operating cash flows. Taxes (at the capital gains tax rate, on the difference between the depreciated property value and the sales price) and the remaining principal mortgage balance are subtracted from the sales price.

$$\text{after-tax sale proceeds} = \text{sales price} - \text{mortgage balance} - \text{tax on gain}$$

$$\text{tax on gain} = \text{capital gains tax rate } [\text{sales price} - (\text{purchase price} - \text{depreciation})]$$

Venture Capital

Stages in *venture capital investing:*

- *Seed stage.* Investors are providing capital in the earliest stage of the business and may help fund research and development of product ideas.
- *Early stage.* Companies are entering operation phase but have yet to produce a market-ready product.
- *Formative stage.* Broad category which encompasses the seed stage and early stage.
- *Later stage.* Marketable goods are in production, and sales efforts are underway, but the company is still privately held.

The following are included within the *later stage*:

- *Second-stage investing* describes investments in a company that is producing and selling a product but is not yet generating income.
- *Third-stage financing* would fund a major expansion of the company.
- *Mezzanine* or *bridge financing* would enable a company to take the steps necessary to go public.

Hedge Funds

Again, not all the Level I review material related to hedge funds applies directly to a Level II LOS. Read this information as a refresher and then focus on the wording in the Level II LOS for your studies.

Leverage, Risk, and Survivorship Bias

Historically, hedge funds actually hedged risk. Currently, the term is used for many investment strategies that have the form of a private partnership, are largely unregulated, and have an incentive performance fee structure. Many hedge funds have concentrated investments (low diversification) and utilize some type of leverage.

The net return of a hedge fund is calculated by subtracting all manager fees from its gross performance.

Risks associated with hedge funds include the following:

- Illiquidity.
- Potential for mispricing.
- Counterparty credit risk.
- Settlement errors.
- Short covering.
- Margin calls.

Compared to other asset classes, hedge funds tend to have higher returns, lower standard deviation of returns, and higher Sharpe ratios. There are, however, certain biases in reported performance and a smoothing due to value estimation of non-traded assets.

The effect of *survivorship bias* from not reporting the results of failed funds is greater for a hedge fund database than for other asset classes because of the lack of required reporting standards in the industry.

Fund managers tend to cherry pick the information they choose to release, reporting on their more successful funds while not providing information on poorly performing funds. Reported returns for a hedge fund database are therefore overstating performance because of both survivorship bias and cherry picking.

Survivorship bias has the opposite effect on the risk measures of a hedge fund database. Hedge funds with highly volatile returns tend to fail more frequently, and defunct funds are not generally included in the database. Because the database would only include the more stable funds that have survived, the risk measure of hedge funds as an asset class would be understated.

In a *fund of funds* hedge fund, a manager selects a number of hedge funds, and investors purchase interests in the overall fund.

Advantages include diversification and risk reduction, professional selection of included funds, and possible access to closed funds.

Disadvantages are higher fees and the possibility that fund selection will be poor.

FIXED INCOME (STUDY SESSIONS 14 & 15)

The Level II curriculum assumes you remember much of the Level I fixed income material. Review the features of debt securities, particularly the material on embedded options (including puts and calls) and conversion options. The Level II curriculum contains several LOS related to the risks associated with investing in bonds. For example, understanding prepayment risk is critical to mastering the Level II material on mortgage-backed securities.

While you are not required to calculate effective duration or convexity at Level II (you are asked to explain the calculations using the binomial model), you do need to understand the concepts for the material on valuing mortgage-backed and asset-backed securities. And, if you understand the concept behind duration, the Level II material on key rate duration will be more intuitive.

When reading about the types of fixed income debt, focus your attention on mortgage passthrough securities, municipal and corporate bonds, and asset-backed securities.

You will also need to know the following yield spreads: the nominal spread, the Z-spread, and the option-adjusted spread (OAS). Understanding these yield spreads and applying them to analysis situations is often the most challenging topic in Level II fixed income.

You need to know how to value a bond quickly; review that material so you don't lose valuable study time when you start the Level II material on valuing bonds with embedded options. Although you won't be asked to work through a bootstrapping or forward rate calculation problem, we suggest that you at least read through that material as a base for your Level II studies.

FEATURES OF DEBT SECURITIES

Bond Terminology

- The terms under which money is borrowed are contained in an agreement known as the *indenture*. The indenture defines the obligations of and restrictions on the borrower and forms the basis for all future transactions between the lender/investor and the issuer. These terms are known as *covenants* and include both *negative* (prohibitions on the borrower) and *affirmative* (actions that the borrower promises to perform) sections.

- The *term to maturity* (or simply *maturity*) of a bond is the length of time until the loan contract or agreement expires. It defines the (remaining) life of the bond.
- The *par value* of a bond is the amount that the borrower promises to pay on or before the maturity date of the issue.
- The *coupon rate* is the rate that, when multiplied by the par value of a bond, gives the amount of interest to be paid annually by the borrower.

Coupon Structures

- *Zero-coupon bonds* are bonds that do not pay periodic interest. Such bonds do not carry coupons but instead are sold at a deep discount from their par values. Market convention dictates that semiannual compounding should be used when pricing zeros.
- *Accrual bonds* are similar to zero-coupon bonds but are sold originally at par value. There is a stated coupon rate, but the coupon interest builds up at a compound rate until maturity.
- *Step-up notes* have coupon rates that increase over time at a specified rate.
- *Deferred-coupon bonds* carry coupons, but the initial coupon payments are deferred for some period.

Floating-Rate Securities

- Floating-rate securities make varying coupon interest payments which are set based on a specified interest rate or index using the specified coupon formula:

  new coupon rate = reference rate ± quoted margin

- Some floating-rate securities have limits on the coupon rate. An upper limit, which is called a *cap*, puts a maximum on the interest rate paid by the borrower. A lower limit, called a *floor*, puts a minimum on the interest rate received by the lender. When a bond has both a cap and a floor, the combination is called a *collar*.

Embedded Options

A *call feature* gives the bond issuer the right to retire the issue early by paying the call price, which is typically above the face value of the bond at the first call date and declines over time to par. A period of years after issuance for which there is no call allowed is called the period of call protection.

A *prepayment option* is similar to a call feature and gives the issuer of an amortizing (e.g., mortgage) security the right to repay principal ahead of scheduled repayment, in whole or in part.

A *put feature* gives the owner of a bond the right to receive principal repayment prior to maturity.

A *conversion option* gives a bondholder the right to exchange the bond for a specified number of common shares of the issuer. When such an option allows exchange for the common shares of another issuer, it is called an *exchange option*.

An embedded option that benefits the issuer will increase the yield required by bond buyers. An embedded option that benefits the bondholder will decrease the yield required on the bond.

RISKS ASSOCIATED WITH INVESTING IN BONDS

The most important risks associated with investing in bonds are interest rate risk, reinvestment risk, and credit risk.

Interest rate risk. As the rates go up (down), bond prices go down (up). This is the source of interest rate risk, which is approximated by *duration*.

Call risk. Call protection reduces call risk. When interest rates are more volatile, callable bonds have more call risk.

Prepayment risk. If rates fall, causing prepayments to increase, the investor must reinvest at the new lower rate.

Yield curve risk. Changes in the shape of the yield curve mean that yields change by different amounts for bonds with different maturities.

Reinvestment risk. Reinvestment risk occurs when interest rates decline and investors are forced to reinvest bond cash flows at lower yields. Reinvestment risk is the greatest for bonds that have embedded call options, prepayment options, or high coupon rates and is greater for amortizing securities than for non-amortizing securities.

Credit risk. Credit risk comes in three forms: *default risk, credit spread risk,* and *downgrade risk.*

Liquidity risk. Because investors prefer more liquidity to less, a decrease in a security's liquidity will decrease its price, and the required yield will be higher.

Exchange-rate risk. This is the uncertainty about the value of foreign currency cash flows to an investor in terms of his home country currency.

Volatility risk. This risk is present for fixed-income securities that have embedded options: call options, prepayment options, or put options. Changes in interest rate volatility affect the value of these options and thus affect the value of securities with embedded options.

Inflation risk. This is the risk of *unexpected* inflation, also called purchasing power risk.

Event risk. Risks outside the risks of financial markets (e.g., natural disasters, corporate takeovers).

Figure 11: Bond Characteristics and Interest Rate Risk

Characteristic	Interest Rate Risk	Duration
Maturity up	Interest rate risk up	Duration up
Coupon up	Interest rate risk down	Duration down
Add a call	Interest rate risk down	Duration down
Add a put	Interest rate risk down	Duration down

Duration of a Bond

Duration is a measure of a security's price sensitivity to changes in yield. It can be interpreted as an approximation of the percentage change in the bond price for a 1% change in yield. It is the ratio of the percentage change in bond price to the change in yield in percentage.

$$\text{duration} = -\frac{\%\ \text{change in bond price}}{\text{yield change in \%}}$$

To get the approximate percentage bond price change, given its duration and a specific change in yield, use the following formula:

$$\%\ \text{change in bond price} = -\text{duration} \times \text{yield change in \%}$$

OVERVIEW OF BOND SECTORS AND INSTRUMENTS

Securities Issued by the U.S. Department of the Treasury

Treasury securities. Issued by the U.S. Treasury, thus backed by the full faith and credit of the U.S. government. Considered to be credit-risk free.

Treasury bills. T-bills have maturities of less than one year and do not make explicit interest payments, paying only the face (par) value at the maturity date. They are sold at a discount to par, and interest is received when the par value is paid at maturity.

Treasury notes and Treasury bonds. Pay semiannual coupon interest at a rate that is fixed at issuance. Notes have original maturities of 2, 3, 5, and 10 years. Bonds have original maturities of 20 or 30 years.

Treasury STRIPS. Because the U.S. Treasury does not issue zero-coupon notes and bonds, investment bankers began stripping the coupons from Treasuries to create zero-coupon bonds to meet investor demand. These stripped securities are of two types:

- *Coupon strips* are the coupon payments, each of which has been stripped from the original security and acts like a fixed-term zero-coupon bond.
- *Principal strips* refer to the principal payments from stripped bonds.

Federal agency securities. **Agency bonds** are debt securities issued by various agencies and organizations of the U.S. government, such as the Federal Home Loan Bank (FHLB). Most agency issues are *not* obligations of the U.S. Treasury and technically should not be considered to be riskless like Treasury securities. However, they are very high-quality securities that have low risk of default.

Mortgage Passthrough Securities

A *mortgage passthrough security* is created by pooling a large number of mortgages together. Shares are sold in the form of *participation certificates.* Interest, scheduled principal payments, and prepayments are passed through to investors after deducting small administrative and servicing fees. Like the underlying mortgage loans, mortgage passthroughs are *amortizing securities.* Prepayment risk is the risk that homeowners either pay additional principal or pay off the entire loan balance prior to the stated maturity. This typically happens when interest rates are low—so the investor gets more principal back in a low-interest-rate environment.

Collateralized mortgage obligations (CMOs) are created from mortgage passthrough securities. Different tranches (slices) represent claims to different cash flows from the passthrough securities and can have different maturities or different prepayment risk than the original passthrough.

Securities Issued by Municipalities in the United States

The coupon interest on *municipal bonds* is typically exempt from federal taxation in the United States and from state income tax in the state of issuance. Following are two types of municipal bonds (munis):

- *Tax-backed debt* (general obligation bonds) is secured by the full faith and credit of the borrower and is backed by its unlimited taxing authority, which includes the ability to impose individual income tax, sales tax, property tax, or corporate tax.
- *Revenue bonds* are supported only by the revenues generated from projects that are funded with the help of the original bond issue.

To compare tax-exempt with taxable bonds (like corporates), you must convert the tax-exempt yield to a taxable equivalent yield.

$$\text{taxable equivalent yield} = \frac{\text{tax-exempt municipal yield}}{1 - \text{marginal tax rate}}$$

Insured bonds are guaranteed for the life of the issue by a third party.

Pre-refunded bonds have been collateralized with Treasury securities in an amount sufficient to make scheduled interest and principal payments and are considered of the highest quality.

Corporate Bonds

Secured bonds have first claim to specific assets in the event of default.

Unsecured bonds are called *debentures*. Those with first claim to cash flows and to proceeds of asset sales in the event of liquidation are called *senior bonds*.

Junior bonds have a claim after those of senior bonds and are sometimes called *subordinated* bonds or notes. All bonds have priority to cash flows before those of preferred stock and common stock.

Asset-Backed Securities

Asset-backed securities (ABS) are collateralized by financial assets that the corporation has sold to a separate legal entity. They lower borrowing costs when the separate entity (special purpose vehicle) can attain a higher credit rating than the corporation.

With this structure, financial difficulties of the corporation should not affect the ABS credit. Often, credit enhancements in the form of guarantees of another corporation, a bank letter of credit, or bond insurance are employed to further reduce borrowing costs.

Other Debt Instruments

Negotiable CDs are issued in a wide range of maturities by banks, traded in a secondary market, backed by bank assets, and termed Eurodollar CDs when denominated in US$ and issued outside the United States.

Bankers acceptances are issued by banks to guarantee a future payment for goods shipped, are sold at a discount to the future payment they promise, are short term, and have limited liquidity.

Collateralized debt obligations (CDOs) are backed by an underlying pool of debt securities which may be any one of a number of types: corporate bonds, bank loans, emerging markets debt, mortgage-backed securities, or other CDOs.

The primary market in bonds includes underwritten and best-efforts public offerings, as well as private placements. The secondary market in bonds includes some trading on exchanges and a much larger volume of trading in the dealer (OTC) market. Electronic trading networks continue to be an increasingly important part of the secondary market for bonds.

CREDIT SPREADS

Credit spread refers to the *difference in yield between two issues that are identical in all respects except their credit ratings.* Credit spreads are a function of the state of the economy. During economic expansion, credit spreads decline as corporations are expected to have stronger cash flows. During economic contractions, cash flows are pressured, which leads to a greater probability of default and increasing credit spreads.

INTRODUCTION TO THE VALUATION OF FIXED INCOME SECURITIES

Bond Valuation Process

- Estimate the cash flows over the life of the security—coupon payments and return of principal.
- Determine the appropriate discount rate based on risk associated with the estimated cash flows.
- Calculate the present value of the estimated cash flows.

Difficulties in Estimating the Expected Cash Flows

- Timing of principal repayments is not known with certainty.
- Coupon payments are not known with certainty.
- The bond is convertible or exchangeable into another security.

Bond Valuation

Bond prices, established in the market, can be expressed either as a percentage of par value or as a yield. Yield to maturity (YTM) is the single discount rate that will make the present value of a bond's promised semiannual cash flows equal to the market price.

In the United States, bonds typically make coupon payments (equal to one-half the stated coupon rate multiplied by the face value) twice a year, and the yield to maturity is expressed as twice the semiannual discount rate that will make the present value of the semiannual coupon payments equal to the market price. This yield to maturity, calculated for a semiannual-pay bond, is also referred to as a *bond equivalent yield.*

For bonds that make annual payments, the YTM is the annual discount rate that makes the present value of the annual coupon payments equal to the market price. Thus, the relation between an annual and semiannual YTM is:

$$YTM_{annual-pay} = \left(1 + \frac{YTM_{semiannual-pay}}{2}\right)^2 - 1$$

$$YTM_{semiannual-pay} = \left[\left(1 + YTM_{annual-pay}\right)^{\frac{1}{2}} - 1\right] \times 2$$

The relation between the semiannual YTM (the bond equivalent yield) and price for a bond with N years to maturity can be represented as:

$$\text{bond price} = \frac{CPN_1}{\left(1 + \frac{YTM}{2}\right)} + \frac{CPN_2}{\left(1 + \frac{YTM}{2}\right)^2} + \ldots + \frac{CPN_{2N} + Par}{\left(1 + \frac{YTM}{2}\right)^{2N}}$$

The price-yield relationship for a zero-coupon bond with N years to maturity is based on a semiannual yield or bond equivalent yield by convention, so we have:

$$\text{zero-coupon bond price} = \frac{\text{face value}}{\left(1 + \frac{YTM}{2}\right)^{2N}}$$

$$\text{zero-coupon YTM} = \left[\left(\frac{\text{face value}}{\text{price}}\right)^{\frac{1}{2N}} - 1\right] \times 2$$

A bondholder will actually realize the YTM on his initial investment only if all payments are made as scheduled; the bond is held to maturity; and, *importantly,* all interim cash flows are reinvested at the YTM.

Spot Rates and No-Arbitrage Bond Values

A yield curve is a plot of YTM versus bond maturity. We can call that the "par yield curve" if it is constructed with the YTMs for bonds trading at par.

Spot rates are market discount rates for single payments to be received in the future and can be thought of, theoretically, as equivalent to the market yields on zero-coupon bonds. Given the spot-rate yield curve, we can discount each of a bond's promised cash flows at its appropriate spot rate and sum the resulting present values to get the market value of the bond.

Values calculated in this way are called *no-arbitrage values,* and we will present the reason for this terminology shortly. With C_N and S_N being the N-period coupon payments and spot rates respectively, we can write:

$$\text{bond value} = \frac{C_1}{(1 + S_1)^1} + \frac{C_2}{(1 + S_2)^2} + \ldots \ldots \frac{C_N + \text{face}}{(1 + S_N)^N}$$

Government bond dealers can separate Treasury bonds into their pieces (the individual coupon and principal cash flows), a process known as *stripping the bond*. These individual pieces are a series of zero-coupon bonds with different maturity dates, and each can be valued by discounting at the spot rate for the appropriate maturity. Because bond dealers can also recombine a bond's individual cash flows into a bond, arbitrage prevents the market price of the bond from being more or less than the value of the individual cash flows discounted at spot rates.

If the no-arbitrage value is greater than the market price, a bond dealer can buy the bond, strip it, and sell the "pieces" for the greater amount to earn an arbitrage profit. If the market price of the bond is greater than the no-arbitrage value, a dealer can buy the pieces, combine them into a bond, and sell the bond to make a profit.

Figure 12: Relationships Between Different Yield Measures

Bond Selling at	Relationship
Par	coupon rate = current yield = yield to maturity
Discount	coupon rate < current yield < yield to maturity
Premium	coupon rate > current yield > yield to maturity

Bootstrapping Spot Rates

The following example illustrates the concept of bootstrapping spot rates from coupon bond prices using known short-term spot rates.

Example:

A 2-year bond with an 8% annual coupon is priced at 100 and the 1-year spot rate is 4%. Use the bootstrapping method to find the 2-year spot rate.

Answer:

The arbitrage-free pricing relationship is $100 = \dfrac{8}{1.04} + \dfrac{108}{\left(1+Z_2\right)^2}$,

so we can write $100 - 7.6923 = \dfrac{108}{\left(1+Z_2\right)^2}$,

and we solve for Z_2 as $Z_2 = \left(\dfrac{108}{92.3077}\right)^{\frac{1}{2}} - 1 = 8.167\%$.

The idea of bootstrapping is that we can repeat this process sequentially. Given Z_1, Z_2, and the price of a 3-year bond, we could calculate Z_3 in the same manner.

Forward Rates

A forward rate is a rate for borrowing/lending at some date in the future. The key here is that investors should receive the same total return from investing in a 2-year bond as they would if they invested in a 1-year bond and then rolled the proceeds into a second 1-year bond at maturity of the first bond, one year from today.

This idea is shown in the relation between an N-period spot rate and a series of forward 1-year rates. Letting $_1f_0$ be the current 1-year rate and $_1f_N$ be the 1-year rate N years from now, we can write:

$$\text{N-period spot rate } (S_N) = \left[(1 + {_1f_0})(1 + {_1f_1}).......(1 + {_1f_N}) \right]^{\frac{1}{N}} - 1$$

The formula for computing the one-period forward rate n periods from today using spot rates is:

$$_1f_n = \frac{(1 + spot_{n+1})^{n+1}}{(1 + spot_n)^n} - 1$$

The Option-Adjusted Spread (OAS) and Zero-Volatility (Z) Spreads

The *nominal spread* is simply an issue's YTM minus the YTM of a Treasury security of similar maturity. Therefore, the use of the nominal spread suffers from the same limitations as the YTM.

The *static spread* (or *zero-volatility spread*) is not the spread over a single Treasury's YTM, but the spread over each of the spot rates on the spot rate yield curve. In other words, *the same spread is added to all risk-free spot rates* to make the PV of the bond's promised cash flows equal to its market price. The Z-spread is inherently more accurate than (and will usually differ from) the nominal spread, because it is based upon the arbitrage-free spot rates, rather than a given YTM. The Z-spread will equal the nominal spread if the term structure of interest rates (the yield curve) is perfectly flat.

The *option-adjusted spread* is used when a bond has embedded options. It can be thought of as the difference between the static or Z-spread and the option cost.

Z-spread – option-adjusted spread = option cost in %

For a bond with a call feature, the option cost will be positive (you require a higher yield). For a bond with a put feature, the option cost will be negative because a bond with a put feature will have a lower required yield than an identical option-free bond.

The intuition of the OAS is that it is the spread once any differences in yield due to the embedded option are removed. Thus, it is a spread that reflects differences in yield for differences in credit risk and liquidity. That's why it must be used for bonds with embedded options and will be the same as the Z-spread for option-free bonds.

Introduction to the Measurement of Interest Rate Risk

Remember, you are not asked to calculate effective duration or convexity at Level II. However, a quick review of this material may help you with the material on valuing callable bonds and analyzing the interest rate risk of a mortgage-backed or asset-backed security.

Duration is a measure of the *slope* of the price-yield function, which is steeper at low interest rates and flatter at high interest rates. Hence, duration (interest rate sensitivity) is higher at low rates and lower at high rates. This concept holds for noncallable bonds. Convexity is a measure of the degree of curvature of the price/yield relationship. Convexity accounts for the error in the estimated change in a bond's price based on duration.

Figure 13: Price-Yield Function of an Option-Free Bond

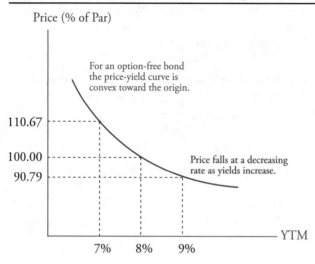

If the bond is callable and the bond is likely to be called, as yields fall, no one will pay a price higher than the call price. The price will not rise significantly as yields fall and you will see *negative convexity* at work. Remember, the verbal description of negative convexity is, "as yields fall, prices rise at a decreasing rate." For a positively convex bond, as yields fall, prices rise at an *increasing* rate.

Figure 14: Price-Yield Function of a Callable Bond

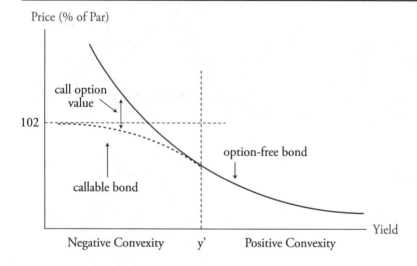

©2011 Kaplan, Inc.

Measuring Interest Rate Risk

There are two approaches to measuring interest rate risk: the full valuation approach (scenario analysis approach) and the duration/convexity approach.

Full valuation or scenario analysis approach:

This approach revalues all bonds in a portfolio under a given interest rate change (yield curve) scenario. It is theoretically preferred and gives a good idea of the change in portfolio value. This method requires accurate valuation models and consists of these steps:

Step 1: Start with current market yield and price.
Step 2: Estimate changes in yields.
Step 3: Revalue bonds.
Step 4: Compare new value to current value.

Duration/convexity approach:

This approach provides an approximation of the actual interest rate sensitivity of a bond or bond portfolio. It has an advantage due to its simplicity compared to the full valuation approach.

The most concise, useful description of *duration is that it represents the sensitivity of a bond's (or portfolio's) price to a 1% change in yield to maturity.*

To use the following formula for effective duration, enter Δy as a decimal (e.g., 0.005 for one-half percent).

$$\text{effective duration} = \frac{\text{value when yield falls by } \Delta y - \text{value when yield rises by } \Delta y}{2 \times \text{beginning value} \times (\Delta y)}$$

The above equation provides a measure which allows us to approximate the percentage change in the price of a bond for a 100 basis point (1.00%) change in yield to maturity.

Modified duration assumes that the cash flows on the bond will not change (i.e., that we are dealing with a noncallable bond). This differs from *effective duration*, which considers expected changes in cash flows that may occur for bonds with embedded options. Effective duration must be used for bonds with embedded options.

Level I Refresher

Modified duration and *effective duration* are good approximations of potential bond price behavior only for relatively small changes in interest rates. As rate changes grow larger, the curvature of the bond price/yield relationship becomes more important. The widening error in the estimated price is due to the curvature of the actual price path, *a bond's convexity.*

The approximate percentage price change is calculated as follows. Use the decimal change in yield here, too.

$$\text{percentage change in price} = \text{duration effect} + \text{convexity effect}$$

$$= \left[-\text{duration} \times (\Delta y)\right] + \left[\text{convexity} \times (\Delta y)^2\right] \times 100$$

The *price value of a basis point* (PVBP) is the dollar change in a portfolio or asset value for a one basis point change in yield.

$$\text{PVBP} = \text{duration} \times 0.0001 \times \text{value}$$

©2011 Kaplan, Inc.

DERIVATIVE INVESTMENTS (STUDY SESSIONS 16 & 17)

The derivatives material is challenging for many Level II candidates. While some other topical areas ease the candidate into the Level II material, the derivatives material starts where the Level I LOS ended. For example, this section on derivatives ends with several call and put payoff diagrams and formulas. Although this material is not specifically tested at Level II, it is assumed you can quickly assess when a call or put option is in or out of the money and that you understand the general mechanics of those options. You are also expected to have a working knowledge of forward contracts, futures contracts, forward rate agreements, swaps, call and put options, and put-call parity.

When reviewing this Level I material, keep in mind that you will not be directly tested on it at Level II, but you will be expected to use the foundation derivative concepts to value forwards, futures, swaps, and embedded options, such as puts and calls. Again, don't waste valuable time memorizing the formulas and diagrams, but make sure you are comfortable with the material before moving on to Level II derivatives.

DERIVATIVE MARKETS AND INSTRUMENTS

A *derivative* is a security that *derives* its value from the value of or return on another asset or security.

Forwards and swaps are typically originated by dealers and have no active secondary market. Futures contracts are originated by and traded in a futures exchange. Some options contracts are traded on an organized options exchange, and others are originated by dealers and do not trade in a secondary market.

Overview of Derivative Contracts

- In a *forward contract,* one party agrees to buy, and the counterparty to sell, a physical asset or a security at a specific price on a specific date in the future. If the future price of the asset increases, the buyer (at the older, lower price) has a gain and the seller a loss.

- A *futures contract* is a forward contract that is standardized and exchange traded. Futures contracts differ from forward contracts in that futures are traded in an active secondary market, are regulated, are backed by the clearinghouse, and require a daily settlement of gains and losses.
- A *swap* is equivalent to a series of forward contracts. In the simplest swap, one party agrees to pay the short-term (floating) rate of interest on some principal amount, and the counterparty agrees to pay a certain (fixed) rate of interest in return. Swaps of different currencies and equity returns are also common.
- An option to buy an asset at a particular price is termed a *call option*. The seller of the option has an *obligation* to sell the asset at the agreed-upon price if the call buyer chooses to exercise the right to buy the asset.
- An option to sell an asset at a particular price is termed a *put option*. The seller of the option has an *obligation* to purchase the asset at the agreed-upon price if the put buyer chooses to exercise the right to sell the asset.

Arbitrage

Arbitrage opportunities arise when assets are mispriced. Trading by arbitrageurs will continue until they affect supply and demand enough to bring asset prices to efficient (no-arbitrage) levels.

There are two arbitrage arguments that are particularly useful in the study and use of derivatives:

- The first is based on the "law of one price." Two securities or portfolios that have identical cash flows in the future, regardless of future events, should have the same price. If A and B have identical future payoffs, and A is priced lower than B, buy A and sell B.
- The second type of arbitrage is used when two securities with uncertain returns can be combined in a portfolio that will have a certain payoff. If a portfolio consisting of A and B has a certain payoff, the portfolio should yield the risk-free rate.

FORWARD MARKETS AND CONTRACTS

Forward Contracts

A *deliverable* forward contract for an asset specifies that the long will pay a certain amount at a specific future date to the short, who will deliver the underlying asset. Neither party pays at contract initiation.

A *cash settlement* forward contract does not require actual delivery of the underlying asset but instead requires a cash payment to the party that is disadvantaged by the difference between the market price of the asset and the contract price at the settlement date.

Early termination of a forward contract can be accomplished by entering into a new forward contract with the opposite position, at the then-current forward price. This early termination will fix the amount of the gains or losses on the forward contract as of the termination date.

Forward contracts are described by the type of asset that must be purchased or sold under the terms of the contract. Equity forwards require delivery or cash settlement based on the value of a stock, a specific portfolio of stocks, or a stock index.

Currency forwards are widely used to hedge exchange rate risk and require delivery of a specified amount of a particular currency with a contract price in another currency.

Bond forwards are often written on zero-coupon bonds with payoffs to the long that increase if rates decrease. A related type of forward contract is a forward rate agreement, where increasing rates increase the payoff to the long position.

Forward Rate Agreements

A *forward rate agreement* (FRA) can be viewed as a forward contract to borrow/lend money at a certain rate at some future date, although it is a cash settlement contract. The long position in an FRA is the party that would borrow the money (long the loan with the contract "price" being the interest rate on the loan). If the floating rate at contract expiration is above the rate specified in the forward agreement, the long position will profit; the contract can be viewed as the right to borrow at below-market rates.

The London Interbank Offered Rate (LIBOR) is a short-term rate based on the rates at which large London banks will lend U.S. dollars to each other. *Euribor* is a similar rate for borrowing and lending in euros.

The payment at settlement on an FRA is the present value of the difference in interest costs between a riskless loan at the market rate and one made at the rate specified in the contract. The difference in rates is multiplied by the notional amount of the contract to get the difference in interest due at the end of the loan term. Because this hypothetical loan would be made at contract settlement, the interest savings or excess interest costs would be paid later, at the end of the loan term. For this reason, the payment at settlement is the present value of the interest difference, discounted at the rate prevailing at settlement.

The general formula for the payment to the long at settlement is:

$$(\text{notional principal}) \left[\frac{(\text{floating rate at settlement} - \text{forward rate})\left(\dfrac{\text{days}}{360}\right)}{1 + \text{floating rate at settlement}\left(\dfrac{\text{days}}{360}\right)} \right]$$

FUTURES MARKETS AND CONTRACTS

Futures vs. Forwards

Figure 15: Key Differences Between Futures and Forwards

Forwards	*Futures*
Private contracts	Exchange traded
Unique customized contracts	Standardized contracts
Default risk is present	Guaranteed by clearinghouse
Little or no regulation	Regulated
No margin deposit required	Margin required and adjusted

Margin

There are three types of futures margin (initial, maintenance, and variation).

The first deposit is called the *initial margin*. Initial margin must be posted before any trading takes place. Initial margin is fairly low and equals about one day's maximum fluctuation in the contract value. The margin requirement is low because at the end of every day, there is a *daily settlement* process called marking to market.

In *marking to market*, any losses for the day are removed from the trader's account, and any gains are added to the trader's account. Thus, any gains or losses in the value of the futures position (futures contract) are realized each day.

If the margin balance in the trader's account falls below a certain level (called the *maintenance margin*), the trader will get a *margin call* and must deposit more cash or securities (called the *variation margin*) into the account to bring the margin balance back up to the initial level. If the margin balance increases above the initial margin amount, the investor can withdraw funds from the account in the amount of the excess above the initial margin requirement.

Futures Contract Basics

Futures contracts specify the quality and quantity of the underlying asset, the delivery or settlement date in the future, and the place of delivery. The futures exchange decides which contracts will be traded, determines the minimum price change, and sets limits on daily price moves.

The Futures Clearing Corporation specifies margin requirements and acts as the counterparty to every trade. Standardization makes the futures contracts quite liquid, so to close out a futures position prior to settlement, a trader can enter into an opposite futures position. The cumulative mark to market in the futures account will have already accounted for any gains or losses on the position prior to the date of the *offsetting or closing trade*.

Most futures contracts are terminated by offsetting trades. Delivery of the asset, cash settlement at contract expiration, or an off-exchange delivery called *exchange for physicals* are the other methods of terminating a futures position.

Some bond futures contracts provide valuable delivery options to the short, which include what bond to deliver and when during the expiration month to deliver.

OPTION MARKETS AND CONTRACTS

Option Terminology and Basics

Call option:

- Long position: *right to buy* the underlying stock at a specific price on a future date.
- Short position: *obligation to sell* the stock to the buyer of the call option.

Put option:

- Long position: *right to sell* the underlying stock at a specific price on a future date.
- Short position: *obligation to buy* the stock from the buyer of the put option.

The *strike price (X)* represents the exercise price specified in the contract.

The seller or short position in an options contract is sometimes referred to as the *writer* of the option.

Stock options are typically on 100 shares of stock.

American options allow the owner to exercise the option at any time before or at expiration.

European options can only be exercised at expiration. For two otherwise identical options, an American option has more flexibility than the European option, so it is worth at least as much and typically more.

Moneyness and Intrinsic Value

An option that would provide a positive payoff if exercised is said to be *in the money*. The *intrinsic value* of an option is the amount that it is in the money, and zero otherwise. The difference between the price of an option (called its premium) and its intrinsic value is termed its *time value*.

The following table summarizes the moneyness of options based on the stock's current price, S, and the option's exercise strike price, X.

Moneyness	Call Option	Put Option
In the money	$S > X$	$S < X$
At the money	$S = X$	$S = X$
Out of the money	$S < X$	$S > X$

- In general, an option is more valuable when its time to expiration is longer and when the price of the underlying asset is more volatile.
- Call options increase in value when the asset price increases, the exercise price is lower, or when the risk-free rate is higher.
- Put options increase in value when the asset price is lower, the exercise price is higher, or when the risk-free rate is lower.
- Both put and call options have greater value when the volatility of the price of the underlying asset is greater.

Interest Rate Options vs. Forward Rate Agreements

For interest rate options, the exercise price is an interest rate, and payoffs depend on a reference rate, such as LIBOR. Interest rate options are similar to forward rate agreements (FRAs) because there is no deliverable asset and they are settled in cash, in an amount based on a notional amount and the difference between the strike rate and the reference rate.

The combination of a long interest rate call option plus a short interest rate put option has the same payoff as an FRA. One difference is that interest rate option payoffs are made after the option expiration date at a date corresponding to the end of the loan period specified in the contract (30-day, 60-day, 90-day LIBOR, etc.). Recall that FRAs pay the present value of this interest difference at settlement.

Other Types of Options

Commodity options are on physical underlying assets, such as gold.

Index option payoffs are based on the difference between the strike price and the index, multiplied by a specified multiplier.

Options on futures give the long the right to enter into a futures position at the futures price specified in the option contract.

Minimum and Maximum Option Values

Figure 16: Lower and Upper Bounds for Options

Option	Minimum Value	Maximum Value
European call	$c_t \geq \text{Max}[0, S_t - X / (1 + \text{RFR})^{T-t}]$	S_t
American call	$C_t \geq \text{Max}[0, S_t - X / (1 + \text{RFR})^{T-t}]$	S_t
European put	$p_t \geq \text{Max}[0, X / (1 + \text{RFR})^{T-t} - S_t]$	$X / (1 + \text{RFR})^{T-t}$
American put	$P_t \geq \text{Max}[0, X - S_t]$	X

Put-Call Parity

Put-call parity means that portfolios with identical payoffs must sell for the same price to prevent arbitrage. A fiduciary call (composed of a call option and a risk-free bond that will pay X at expiration) and a protective put (composed of a share of stock and a long put) both have identical payoffs at maturity. Based on this fact and the law of one price, we can state that, for European options:

$$C + X / (1 + RFR)^T = S + P$$

Each of the individual securities in the put-call parity relationship can be expressed as:

$$S = C - P + X / (1 + RFR)^T$$

$$P = C - S + X / (1 + RFR)^T$$

$$C = S + P - X / (1 + RFR)^T$$

$$X / (1 + RFR)^T = S + P - C$$

The single securities on the left side of the equations all have exactly the same payoffs at expiration as the portfolios on the right side. The portfolios on the right side are the "synthetic" equivalents of the securities on the left. Note that the options must be European style, and the puts and calls must have the same exercise prices for these relations to hold.

The four relations all must hold to prevent arbitrage; if there is a profitable arbitrage opportunity, *all of these relations* will be violated. If the equality does not hold, buy the "cheap" side of the equation and sell the other "expensive" side. This will produce an immediate *arbitrage profit*.

SWAP MARKETS AND CONTRACTS

One way to view a swap contract is as an exchange of loans. A simple fixed-for-floating rate swap is equivalent to one party borrowing from another at a fixed rate and the other party borrowing the same amount from the first party and paying a floating rate of interest on the loan. If the loans are in different currencies, it's a currency swap; if one of the loans requires the payment of a rate determined by the return on a stock, portfolio, or index, it is termed an equity swap.

Characteristics of Swap Contracts

- No payment required by either party at initiation except the principal values exchanged in currency swaps.
- Custom instruments.
- Not traded in any organized secondary market.
- Largely unregulated.
- Default risk is a critical aspect of the contracts.
- Institutions dominate.

Methods of Terminating a Swap

- Mutual termination.
- Offsetting swap contract.
- Resale to a third party.
- Exercising a swaption—an option to enter into an offsetting swap.

Currency Swaps

In a currency swap, one party makes payments denominated in one currency, while the payments from the counterparty are made in a second currency. Typically, the notional amounts of the contract, expressed in both currencies, are exchanged at contract initiation and returned at the contract termination date in the same amounts. The periodic interest payments in each of the two currencies can be based on fixed or floating rates.

The cash flows that would occur in a currency swap are as follows:

- Unlike an interest rate swap, the notional principal actually changes hands at the beginning of the swap.
- Interest payments are made without netting. *Full interest payments in two different currencies are exchanged at each settlement date.*
- At the termination of the swap agreement (maturity), the counterparties return the notional amounts. *Notional principal is swapped again at the termination of the agreement.*

Plain Vanilla Interest Rate Swaps

The *plain vanilla interest rate swap* involves trading fixed interest rate payments for floating-rate payments (paying fixed and receiving floating).

The parties involved in any swap agreement are called the *counterparties.*

- The counterparty that wants variable-rate interest agrees to pay fixed-rate interest and is thus called the *pay-fixed* side of the swap.

- The counterparty that receives the fixed payment and agrees to pay variable-rate interest is called the *receive-fixed* or *pay-floating* side of the swap.

Let's look at the cash flows that occur in a plain interest rate swap.

- Because the notional principal swapped is the same for both counterparties and is denominated in the same currency units, there is no need to actually exchange the cash.
- The determination of the variable interest rate is at the beginning of the settlement period, and the cash interest payment is made at the end of the settlement period. This is called payment in *arrears*. Because the interest payments are in the same currency, there is no need for both counterparties to actually transfer the cash. The difference between the fixed-rate payment and the variable-rate payment is calculated and paid to the appropriate counterparty. *Net interest is paid by the party who owes it.*
- At the conclusion of the swap, only the final net payment is made because the notional principal was not swapped.

You should note that swaps are a zero-sum game. What one party gains, the other party loses.

Interest Rate Swap Terminology

- The time frame covered by the swap is called the *tenor* of the swap.
- The *settlement dates* are when the interest payments are to be made.
- The amount used to calculate the payment streams to be exchanged is called the *notional principal*.
- The floating rate quoted is *generally LIBOR flat* or LIBOR plus a spread.

Swap Interest Payments

The basic formula for the net fixed-rate payment in an interest rate swap is:

$$\begin{pmatrix} \text{net fixed-rate} \\ \text{payment} \end{pmatrix}_t = \begin{pmatrix} \text{swap fixed} \\ \text{rate} - \text{LIBOR}_{t-1} \end{pmatrix}\begin{pmatrix} \dfrac{\text{number of days}}{360} \end{pmatrix}\begin{pmatrix} \text{notional} \\ \text{principal} \end{pmatrix}$$

- If this number is positive, the fixed-rate payer *owes* a net payment to the floating-rate party.
- If this number is negative, then the fixed-rate payer *receives* a net payment from the floating-rate party.

In a swap, the floating-rate payment is made based on what the floating rate was at the *beginning* of the settlement period. Hence, when a swap is negotiated (beginning of first period), the net cash payment at the end of the first period is already known. However, the cash flows for all other periods are indeterminate as of the start of the swap and are based on future values of the floating rate.

Equity Swaps

In an equity swap, the return on a stock, a portfolio, or a stock index is paid each period by one party in return for a fixed payment. The return can be the capital appreciation or the total return including dividends on the stock or portfolio. The payment is calculated as the percentage return on the equity over the period multiplied by the notional amount of the swap.

In an equity swap, the first payment (and the others) are unknown, and the fixed-rate payer may actually pay more than the fixed rate if the equity return is negative over the period. It may help to remember that the party that pays equity returns would receive a fixed return on the equity portfolio combined with the swap, regardless of the equity portfolio performance.

RISK MANAGEMENT APPLICATIONS OF OPTION STRATEGIES

The key here is interpreting option payoff diagrams.

- Buyer of a call option—long position.
- Writer (seller) of a call option—short position.
- Buyer of a put option—long position.
- Writer (seller) of a put option—short position.

Call Option Payoff Diagrams

The following graph illustrates the payoff at expiration for a call option as a function of the stock price, for both buyers and writers. Note that this differs from the *profit diagram* that follows in that the profit diagram reflects the initial cost of the option (the *premium*). Remember that the option buyer pays the premium to the option seller and if the option finishes out of the money, the writer keeps the premium and the buyer loses the premium. Options are considered a *zero-sum game* because whatever amount the buyer gains, the seller loses, and vice versa.

intrinsic value of a call option = max[0, S − X]

intrinsic value of a put option = max[0, X − S]

Figure 17: Call Option Payoff Diagram

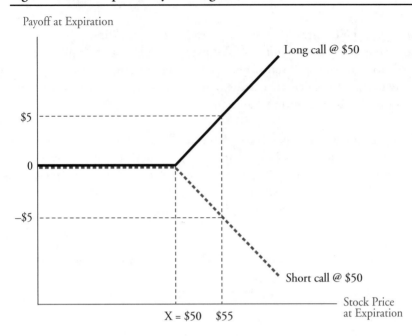

Figure 18: Profit/Loss Diagram for a Call Option

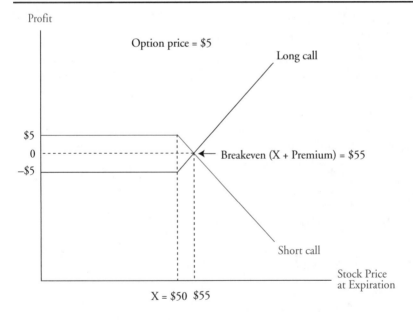

©2011 Kaplan, Inc.

For a *call option:*

$$\text{breakeven}_{call} = \text{strike price} + \text{premium}$$

	Call Option	
	Maximum Loss	*Maximum Gain*
Buyer (long)	Premium	Unlimited
Seller (short)	Unlimited	Premium
Breakeven	X + premium	

Put Option Diagrams

The following graph illustrates the payoff at expiration for a put option as a function of stock price, for both buyers and writers.

Figure 19: Put Option Payoff Diagram

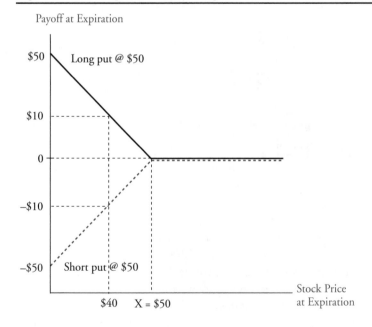

Note that in the *profit diagram* that follows, the cost of the option (the *premium*) is included.

Figure 20: Profit/Loss Diagram for a Put Option

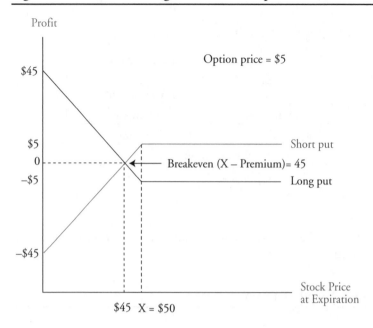

For a *put option:*

	Put Option	
	Maximum Loss	*Maximum Gain*
Buyer (long)	Premium	X – premium
Seller (short)	X – premium	Premium
Breakeven	X – premium	

Covered Calls, Protective Puts

A *covered call* is the combination of a long stock and a short call. The term *covered* means that the stock covers the inherent obligation assumed in writing the call. Why would you write a covered call? You feel the stock's price will not go up any time soon, and you want to increase your income by collecting some call option premiums. This strategy for enhancing income is not without risk. The call writer is trading the stock's upside potential above the strike price for the call premium.

A *protective put* is an investment management technique designed to protect a stock from a decline in value. It is constructed by buying a stock and put option on that stock. Any gain on the stock at option expiration is reduced by the put premium paid. The combined (protective put) position will produce profits at

©2011 Kaplan, Inc.

option expiration only if the stock price exceeds the sum of the purchase prices of the stock and the put. If the stock price at option expiration is below the put's strike price, the put payoff will limit the maximum loss to the difference between the cost of the position and the strike price of the put.

PORTFOLIO MANAGEMENT (STUDY SESSION 18)

Nearly all the Level I portfolio management curriculum carries over to Level II, either directly or indirectly. At Level II, you will be tested on the importance of the investment policy statement and expected to be able to define investor objectives and constraints. Covariance and correlation, the corresponding diversification benefits, as well as the Markowitz efficient frontier and asset pricing models are important parts of the first topic review at Level II. Review the Level I material on the CML and the SML carefully (including the equation for the SML and the CAPM).

PORTFOLIO MANAGEMENT AND CONSTRUCTION

Importance of Investment Policy Statement

Understand the basic inputs to an investment policy statement and how these inputs relate to individuals, pensions, and endowments.

- The policy statement requires that risks and costs of investing, as well as the return requirements, all be objectively and realistically articulated.
- The policy statement imposes investment discipline on, and provides guidance for, both the client and the portfolio manager.

The investment policy statement should include the following:

Investment objectives

- Return objectives.
- Risk tolerance.

Constraints

- Liquidity needs.
- Time horizon.
- Tax concerns.
- Legal and regulatory factors.
- Unique needs and preferences.

Return Objectives

Capital preservation. Earning a return at least equal to the inflation rate.

Capital appreciation. Earning a *nominal* return that exceeds the inflation rate. Purchasing power of the initial investment increases over time, through capital gains.

Current income. Investments with dividend and/or interest income, generally to pay living expenses or some other planned spending need.

Total return. Objective of having a portfolio grow in value to meet a future need through both capital gains and the reinvestment of current portfolio income.

Factors That Affect an Investor's Risk Tolerance

- Investor's psychological makeup.
- Investor's personal factors, including age, family situation, existing wealth, insurance coverage, current cash reserves, and income.

PORTFOLIO RISK AND RETURN

A risk-averse investor prefers higher to lower expected returns for the same level of expected risk and prefers lower to higher risk for a given level of expected returns. There is a positive relationship between expected returns and risk.

Expected rate of return on a risky asset from *historical* data is the mean (arithmetic average) of all the historical returns.

$$\text{expected return } E(R) = \overline{R} = \frac{R_1 + R_2 + R_3 + \ldots + R_N}{N}$$

Variance of returns from *historical* data is the average squared difference between each observed return and the expected (mean) return.

$$\text{variance} = \sigma^2 = \frac{\sum_{t=1}^{N} (R_t - \overline{R})^2}{N}$$

In either case:

$$\text{standard deviation} = \sigma = \sqrt{\sigma^2}$$

Covariance and Correlation

Covariance measures the extent to which two variables move together over time. The covariance is an absolute measure of movement and is measured in return units squared.

Using *historical data*, we multiply each variable's deviation from its mean by the other variable's deviation from its mean for each period, add them all up, and divide by the number of (paired) observations.

$$cov_{1,2} = \frac{\sum_{t=1}^{N}\left[\left(R_{t,1} - \overline{R}_1\right)\left(R_{t,2} - \overline{R}_2\right)\right]}{N-1}$$

Covariance can be standardized by dividing by the product of the standard deviations of the two securities. This standardized measure of co-movement is called their *correlation coefficient* or *correlation* and is computed as:

$$\text{correlation of assets 1 and 2} = \rho_{1,2} = \frac{cov_{1,2}}{\sigma_1\sigma_2}, \text{ so that } cov_{1,2} = \rho_{1,2}\sigma_1\sigma_2$$

Risk and Return for a Portfolio of Risky Assets

When risky assets are combined into a portfolio, the expected portfolio return is a weighted average of the asset returns, where the weights are the percentages of the total portfolio value invested in each asset.

The standard deviation of returns for a portfolio of risky assets depends on the standard deviations of each asset's return (σ); the proportion of the portfolio in each asset (w); and, crucially, on the covariance or correlation of returns between each asset pair in the portfolio.

Portfolio standard deviation for a two-asset portfolio:

$$\sigma_p = \sqrt{w_1^2\sigma_1^2 + w_2^2\sigma_2^2 + 2w_1w_2\sigma_1\sigma_2\rho_{12}}$$

which is equivalent to:

$$\sigma_p = \sqrt{w_1^2\sigma_1^2 + w_2^2\sigma_2^2 + 2w_1w_2cov_{12}}$$

Efficient Frontier

The Markowitz efficient frontier represents the set of portfolios that have the highest expected return for a given level of risk and the least risk for a given level of expected return, where risk is measured as standard deviation of returns.

An individual investor's optimal (most preferred) portfolio is the risk return combination represented by the point on the efficient frontier that lies on the investor's highest (most preferred) indifference curve. As shown in the following figure, a more risk-averse investor will choose a point like X, compared to a less risk-averse investor who will choose a riskier portfolio, such as Y.

Figure 21: Locating the Optimal Portfolio

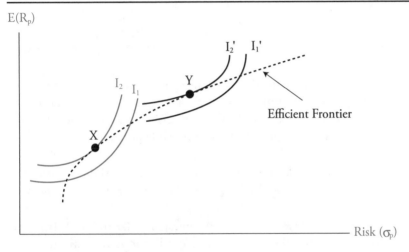

Assumptions of Capital Market Theory

- All investors use the Markowitz mean-variance framework to select securities and, therefore, select only portfolios that lie on the efficient frontier.
- There is unlimited lending and borrowing at the risk-free rate.
- Investors have identical expectations.
- There is a one-period horizon.
- Divisible assets—all assets are infinitely divisible.
- Markets are frictionless—no taxes or transaction costs.
- There is no inflation (or perfectly anticipated inflation).
- Interest rates are constant.
- Capital markets are in equilibrium.

When a risk-free asset is combined with a risky asset in a portfolio, varying the proportions of the two assets results in a set of risk-return combinations that lie on a straight line. The following figure illustrates the possible risk-return combinations from combining a risk-free asset with three different (efficient) portfolios, X, Y, and M.

Figure 22: Combining a Risk-Free Asset With a Risky Portfolio

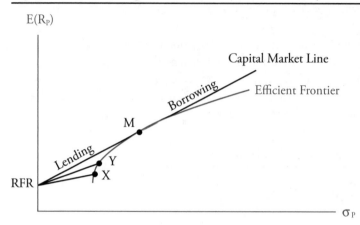

This figure also illustrates the point that combining a risk-free asset with risky Portfolio M (the *tangency* portfolio) results in the best available combination of risk and return. Combining the risk-free asset with either risky Portfolio X or risky Portfolio Y results in a less preferred set of possible portfolios.

Because investors who hold risky assets will choose to hold Portfolio M, it must contain *all* available risky assets, and we can describe it as the *market portfolio.*

Investors at Point M have 100% of their funds invested in Portfolio M. Between R_f and M, investors hold both the risk-free asset and Portfolio M. This means investors are *lending* some of their funds at the risk-free rate and investing the rest in the risky market Portfolio M. To the right of M, investors hold more than 100% of Portfolio M. This means they are *borrowing* funds to buy more of Portfolio M. The *levered positions* represent a 100% investment in Portfolio M and borrowing to invest even more in Portfolio M.

In short, adding a risk-free asset to the set of risky assets considered in the Markowitz portfolio theory results in a new efficient frontier that is now a straight line—the capital market line (CML).

Security Market Line Revisited: Systematic and Unsystematic Risk

Recall the CAPM equation:

$$E(R_i) = RFR + beta_i \times [E(R_{MKT}) - RFR]$$

Under the assumptions of capital market theory, diversification is costless, and investors will only hold efficient portfolios. The risk that is eliminated by diversification is called *unsystematic risk* (also referred to as unique, diversifiable, or firm-specific risk). Because unsystematic risk can be eliminated at no cost, investors need not be compensated in equilibrium for bearing unsystematic risk.

The risk that remains in efficient portfolios is termed *systematic risk* (also referred to as non-diversifiable or market risk), which is measured by an asset's or portfolio's beta. Therefore, we conclude that only systematic or market risk requires additional expected returns in equilibrium. This crucial result is the basis for the capital asset pricing model (CAPM). The equilibrium relationship between systematic risk and expected return is illustrated by the SML.

The *total risk* (standard deviation of returns) for any asset or portfolio of assets can be separated into systematic and unsystematic risk.

total risk = systematic + unsystematic risk

Well-diversified (efficient) portfolios have no unsystematic risk, and a risk-free asset has no systematic (market) risk either. Systematic risk is measured in units of market risk referred to as the beta of an asset or portfolio, so that the beta of the market portfolio is equal to one. The market portfolio simply has one "unit" of market risk.

Figure 23: Security Market Line

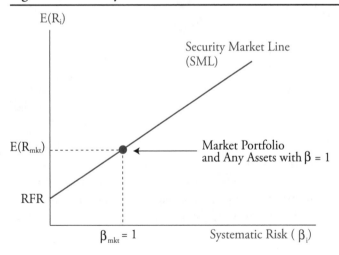

Note that required return and expected return are the same in equilibrium.

 Professor's Note: For Level II, you are not required to use the SML to identify under- and overpriced securities. We included it because understanding the SML is critical to mastering the Level II curriculum, but make sure you focus on the Level II LOS.

An analyst may identify assets for which his forecasted returns differ from the expected return based on the asset's beta. Assets for which the expected return differs from equilibrium expected returns will plot either above or below the SML.

Consider three stocks, A, B, and C, that are plotted on the SML based on their forecasted returns.

Figure 24: Identifying Mispriced Securities

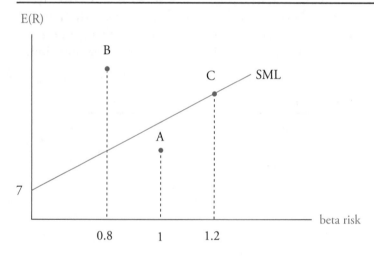

Asset B plots above the SML, so it is underpriced. The interpretation is that the forecasted return is greater than the return necessary to compensate for the asset's systematic risk in equilibrium. A higher-than-equilibrium return implies a lower-than-equilibrium price. Asset A is *overpriced,* by the same reasoning, and Asset C is priced at its equilibrium value.

INDEX

A

accounting equation 31
accounts 30
accounts payable 36
accounts receivable 35
accrual accounting 32
accrual method 34
accrued liabilities 36
amortization 33
amortization expense 33
assets 28

B

balance sheet 28

C

call option 89
call option payoff 87
cash flow statement 29, 39
classified balance sheet 34
common-size format 42
comprehensive income 33
contra accounts 30
contributed capital 38
covered call 90
current assets 34, 35
current liabilities 34, 36

D

degree of financial leverage (DFL) 51
degree of operating leverage (DOL) 51
depreciation 33
double-entry accounting 32

E

equity swap 87
expenses 28, 31
extended DuPont equation 46

F

fair value 35
financial statement elements 30
financial statement notes 29

financing activities 40
financing cash flows 29, 42
free cash flow 42
free cash flow to equity (FCFE) 42
free cash flow to the firm (FCFF) 42
fundamental accounting equation 29

G

gains and losses 28
goodwill 37, 50

H

historical cost 35

I

income statement 28
intangible assets 33, 37, 50
inventories 36
investing cash flows 29, 42

L

liabilities 28, 30
liquidity-based format 34

M

Management's Commentary 29
Management's Discussion and Analysis
   (MD&A) 29
marketable securities 36
matching principle 33

N

noncash investing 40
noncontrolling interest 35, 38
noncurrent assets 35
noncurrent liabilities 35
notes payable 36

O

operating cash flows 29, 41
option strategies 87
owners' equity 29, 31, 38

Index

Notes

Notes

Notes

Notes

Notes

Notes

Notes

Notes

Notes

Notes

Notes